An Accidental Family

Cheryl Moran

Copyright © 2021 by Cheryl Moran

All rights reserved. No part of this publication may be reproduced, distributed, or transmitted in any form or by any means, including photocopying, recording, or other electronic or mechanical methods, without the prior written permission of the publisher, except in the case brief quotations embodied in critical reviews and other noncommercial uses permitted by copyright law.

ISBN: 978-1-63945-016-9 (Paperback)

The views expressed in this book are solely those of the author and do not necessarily reflect the views of the publisher, and the publisher hereby disclaims any responsibility for them.

Writers' Branding
1800-608-6550
www.writersbranding.com
orders@writersbranding.com

Contents

Chapter 1 1
Chapter 2 13
Chapter 3 27
Chapter 4 41
Chapter 5 53
Chapter 6 64
Chapter 7 74
Chapter 8 84
Chapter 9 94
Chapter 10 105
Chapter 11 119

Chapter 1

Money can't buy everything, but it helps. It shows one is successful in business, if not anywhere else. It takes money to make money. Mason and Mandi Morgan were very successful in business. Every venture they made tripled itself in the first year. All over the United States, they were well known among the who's who.

But, was their marriage suffering because of their work? Were they working too much and forgetting each other?

They worked well together in business, had always complimented each other and succeeded.

Mason was the guy-next-door-type, clean-cut, good-looking-but not extremely handsome. Unless you asked Mandi, she thought he was so handsome, her prince.

Mandi was five-six to Mason's six-one; her hair more blonde than his light brown wavy locks. Her eyes were green as summer grass while his were more hazel taking on blue, green, or brown depending on his shirts.

Since Mason played football all though high school and college, he had a strong athletic build which he kept in shape. Mandi was slender with no worries about weight…yet.

They were both still young she at thirty and he at thirty-three. Business savvy adults who happened to be married since their college days, hence, her worries about their future spun from this preoccupation with only business.

"I'll make you a business deal, Mason, "Mandi said one evening as they were both engrossed in their separate lap top dealings.

"And what is that, my dear?" Mason inquired, looking up from the spreadsheet on his computer. The wrinkles across his forehead said he'd been deeply involved in his work, trying to find an answer to a problem.

He was thoughtful, giving him a smile, "I want what we had when we first married. I want adventure and excitement. Can you still give me those two things, my dear, can you, Mason?" she inquired.

Studying her serious look, he replied, "I think I still can, my dear. How do you propose we seal this deal of yours?" He smiled at her. She was the smartest, most beautiful woman he knew. His desire and love for her hadn't dissipated in the past ten years; it had grown.

"How about a get-away, a vacation," she suggested. She had been thinking for a week about what they needed. "I've heard these things work for couples. We have been married ten years and have never taken one. What do you think?"

"Hmm," he began, his brows drawing together "Sounds tempting, but we're just in the middle of settling a few company buy-outs. How do we put that into a vacation?" His eyes were drawn back to the spreadsheet on his computer, figures he was trying to balance.

"Darling, why don't we visit those buy-outs as part of our vacation? We could use one of those bugs RV's from that company we bought last year and take our time."

His mind had returned to his figure-balancing act, while she began to think and plan.

"I've got it, "she said interrupting him again.

"What have you got, my dear?" came his absent-minded response.

"Our vacation plan; we will visit some of the new sites and see other new sites as we do so."

"How many are you talking about?" He could think of a few but didn't relish the thought of living out of an RV for long.

What did she have in mind? "Well… we'll each make a list of our latest deals and compare them." She was getting excited.

He thought: maybe she had a good idea. She'd had so many in the years since they'd formed their company together. Her business sense equaled his; he'd given her that from day one. So, he figured he would accept her deal and travel.

"Traveling does sound interesting, my dear. These three new buy-outs are my list. Let me hear yours." Giving in to her was easy. She named them and they looked at a map: marking out six visits in six different states was the result. They then decided to stretch it out and visit a few extra sites that they would pass nearby on their trip. By bedtime they had their travels all mapped out. It was hard to relax and sleep but they finally did.

As usual, they were up by six the next morning. Each found they were very excited about the prospect of this new adventure.

After breakfast, they went to the RV business they had purchased a year ago and chose the biggest, most luxurious one on the lot for themselves. Mason drove it all over town to get the feel of the machine while Mandi packed clothes and bought food.

By noon they had rearranged their in town schedules, packed the RV with their laptops, clothes, food, and other essentials, and headed out of town.

"This is just like a honeymoon, my dear," Mandi said as she sat in the passenger seat, as excited as a teenager.

They drove until they were tired of sitting and hunger gnawed at them, ate lunch, and then ventured out to find the first business on their agenda.

WEDNESDAY

The trip had been uneventful, visiting each business as they followed the destinations laid out on their map, spending little time at each location as things were running smoothly. It was at their final destination that their world would be turned upside down.

The couple they had just bought one of their latest businesses from had just passed away in a bad car accident. Mason and Mandi arrived the morning of the double funeral honoring a man and his wife of eighteen years.

Out of respect, they attended the funeral. And…found out the couple had five teenage sons who were now orphaned and alone. As usual many people brought food to their home and stayed to visit-more with each other than the boys. But the boys had young people there with the adults, so they weren't really alone. Mason and Mandi were so there, watching, thinking.

Mason introduced himself to the lads before the day was half over, telling them he and his wife had purchased the company form their parents.

The oldest son made a comment, "We have to find a place to live." Visitors were starting to leave the home and the boys found reality setting in.

Mason was confused. His memory seldom failed him.

"What about your home here? I believe your father told me it was paid for. Is there no one to help you?"

Seventeen-year-old Mitchell, the oldest of the five offspring replied, "Sir, Dad's lawyer said the home has to be sold to pay for the funeral and the hospital bills. That's all I know. So…we have to move…somewhere."

"How do we stay together? Who will help all of us?" Mitchell had never had any worries of this nature before in his carefree life.

With everyone leaving them, Mitchell began worrying about the future for him and his four brothers. How would they stay together? Who would help them? Where would they live? And how?

Somehow he voiced his fears out loud to this man who took the time to really listen to him. A stranger. The other people who had brought food and visited were all superficial, visiting, paying their respects like good friends and neighbors, but then leaving and not really helping. Leaving all five of them to fend for themselves, no one worried about the boys after the funeral-except these two strangers.

The five young men were all dressed in nice, well-fitting suits for the funeral. They all had decent haircuts, seemed to be well cared for. Each had dark blond tresses, deep chocolate eyes and tanned olive skin tones.

Taken back, Mason said, "Wait a minute. What has happened to the five-hundred –thousand –dollars that I paid your father for the business?" Mason was totally confused now. How could that much money disappear so fast? It hadn't even cleared his bank, not before they left home anyway.

Now it was Mitchell's turn to be confused as the boys knew nothing about their father's business. "What money, sir? We don't know anything about any check. There's very little in mom and dad's checking account. That's all we know, all the lawyer told us. We know that dad sold the business. He did say he was retiring, but that's all. He never talked about it" Mitchell admitted.

"Well, I promise you I will find out. Could you please give the name of the lawyer?" Mason asked.

As the lad went in search of the lawyer's name and phone number, his mind was on the money. That was a lot of money. Where could it be? That much money could mean him and his brothers could stay in their home, finish school here. Returning, he said to Mr. Morgan, "The lawyer's name is Carl Braxton and here is his phone number. He won't care if you call him, I guess."

Mandi took a different approach, her concern genuine, "Who's here to help you? No one's stayed to help out."

Like all teenagers, Mitchell was sure they could handle it. He shrugged. "No one's needed, ma'am, we will be just fine. We aren't little kids. We don't need anyone. Thank you. Really, we will be just fine."

Mitchell's mind was on the ways to keep them all together. That's all he cared about. His brother, Kyler was sixteen; he and Mitch could both get part time jobs if they needed to stretch the money. They could all stick together and make it work, somehow, Mitch knew the others felt the same-no one wanted to lose a brother. They'd already lost their parents.

"If you'll excuse me, sir, I need to see what's left for supper. I'm sure my brothers are hungry. I know people brought food, but people stayed also, so I'm not sure what's left."

Mandi tried again, "would you let me help?"

Mitch eyed her suspiciously. Then, because none of them had ever cooked-they'd reheated food only-he nodded. He would appreciate the help as he was tired and the day had been hard to get through. Because Mitchell was over-tired, over-stressed with the death of his parents, the funeral, and all the people in and out, stressing him out even more, he accepted Mandi's offer to help.

"Mom always did all the cooking," he explained. "I can reheat food in the microwave, but…," he shrugged. "We will be fine, ma'am, my brothers will help."

"Mitchell, I'd be glad to help you. Just show me the way to the kitchen," Mandi offered.

Sighing, he said, "Yes, ma'am," as he led the way.

Mason found the other four siblings in the family room, engrossed in a movie; they wouldn't be much help to Mitchell tonight, Mason mused as he joined them. He made light conversation during the commercials and found the boys friendly, well-adjusted teens even though they were upset over just losing their parents. They seemed unperturbed that he was there with them. Or, Mason reasoned, did his presence reassure them in some way? And, how could he, a stranger be reassuring?

The table was full of quite a few choices, reheated and ready. Mitchell called his brothers in to eat and they came mutely obeying, their nerves as frayed as his. Watching them eat, Mason hoped there was enough food. The funeral hadn't affected their appetites; they had hollow legs to fill as his grandmother used to say.

All the boys had been through turmoil today and the days since the accident, with all the people in and out, the worry over the home, and the fear of being separated. It took Mitch little prodding to get his two younger sibs to head upstairs, take their showers and go to bed. They were ready. Was Mitchell used to taking over, Mason wondered. Or, was he feeling the weight of responsibility rested on him now? At seventeen, that was a big load to carry.

Mandi had helped Mitch out with the meal and the clean-up. He accepted her help easily and in doing so, accepted Mason being around also. Mason wasn't bossy, he was just there to lean on if Mitch needed him or that's how Mitch felt.

"Are you leaving?" Mitch asked when the ten o'clock news came on and Mason urged the middle two boys to take their showers. They did so willingly.

"Do you want us to stay and help you, Mitchell?" Mason offered. "I do intend to do some research tomorrow on that missing money. I want to find that check."

Mitch felt awkward. He had just met this couple, but somehow he felt an alliance there, a connection he needed right now. His brothers had him to lean on. Who did he have? So, he just nodded. Yes, he wanted them; these strangers who were more help than anyone had been, to stay. Knowing someone was near was a relief he couldn't understand or explain.

"Our RV is out front. We'll be that close, if you need us," Mason assured him.

That wasn't enough. "Uh…you could sleep in mom and dad's room. It won't bother us, really." Mitch felt childish wanting these adults close. He'd always had his parents close. He wasn't sure he was ready to be the parent to his four siblings. In the morning he'd be okay, maybe, but now he needed the support. The security. How did he explain that?

Mason and Mandi exchanged a look. Only that look communicated their decision.

"Okay, only if it won't upset any of you, we'll stick around." He watched relief relax the boy's tired features.

Mandi went out to the RV and brought in what they would need for tonight and in the morning,

"Did your dad keep any business related papers here at home?" Mason asked casually as he waited for the teen to lock up.

The lad wrinkled his face in thought "There's a desk in the family room in the corner where dad kept everything for the home and business, but I don't know what's there. Dad's stuff was always off limits to us," he explained.

Mason nodded. He understood. The man thought he'd live a lot longer, and the boys didn't need to be burdened-yet.

"Tomorrow, I'd like to look through those papers, of you don't mind." Mason's business mind was awhirl, wondering where that check could be.

Mitch shrugged, not sure if this man would find anything worthwhile, said "Okay, if they have anything to do with the business, I guess they're yours anyway."

Mitch knew his brothers would not be against these two staying the night, even in their parent's room because they were as distraught as he was. Tomorrow they would have to sit down and plan out their future, somehow find a solution. Their lives were forever changed .Mitch thought he could no longer be a carefree teenager and his brother Kyler at sixteen would probably feel the same when they all shared and planned. That was tomorrow. Tonight he was going to sleep.

THURSDAY

As usual, Mason and Mandi were up, showered, dressed, and ready to face the day by six A.M. Mandi drove the RV and found a donut shop where she loaded up on different kinds, at least three dozen, while Mason cleaned out the desk and downloaded any business information onto his computer. Drinking coffee, enjoying the donuts, Mason and Mandi were in their normal business mode when, between eight and nine, five young men dragged themselves into the kitchen. Hunger drew them.

Some surprise registered as the younger four found the couple still in their home .Was it still their home? But, acceptance came with the donuts which they devoured along with a whole gallon of milk.

"Mitchell, you will be glad to know that I found the check in your dad's desk. He hadn't deposited it yet." Mitch was glad to hear this, also glad that this man was an honest man. A dishonest man could have destroyed the check and left the boys destitute.

"I've contacted the lawyer also, Mason continued, "I'd like you to come with me and meet the lawyer at the bank. Can you, will you do that?" Mason had been very busy-the desk was almost empty, all cleaned out. He'd also found the parent's checkbook with all the account information for Mitchell.

Mitch smiled a smile of relief. He had found the check-a huge check. They were saved. "Yes, sir," he said, "I'll go with you. We can take mom's minivan instead of your RV. Is that better?"

"Much. Thanks, Mitchell."

Last night when this boy had said "Goodnight," Mason had felt a strong urge to say, "Goodnight, son." Why, he didn't know. They weren't his sons, not one of them, but he felt a deep rooted responsibility for their well-being, their future. He wanted them to have security, not despair.

Mitch couldn't have been happier. This man had found the check; a huge check that could solve many of their problems. Could this be their salvation and the answer to their keeping their home? "Thank you for finding that check. We didn't know of its existence, nor did the lawyer. We won't lose our home now, will we?" Relief and joy were mixed in his voice.

Mason shook his head. "We should be able to take care of everything. I've talked to the lawyer about your future. Together we'll get everything in order. After breakfast, so, eat up…enjoy-there's plenty, I'm sure."

"Yeah, I can see that. Thanks." All five echoed similar comments, appreciative of the donuts.

"Can we all come along?" the youngest Aiden asked. He was thirteen.

"I can't see why not if the car will hold all of us," Mason answered.

"Duh, of course it will, "Aiden told him, "How do you think our mom took care of all of us?"

Mason smiled, of course," he conceded, new at this.

At the bank they met with the assistant manager and their parent's lawyer in the assistant manager's private office. The bank manager didn't want to put a seventeen-year-old in charge of that enormous amount of money as he did not have legal custody of his brothers and he was inexperienced with handling affairs of any kind as yet. There might be problems and repercussions.

Mason knew, as well as the bank manager that Mitchell needed to be eighteen to legally be the custodial guardian for his brothers, but that there were sometimes ways to get around that, also legally. This was what he had at first thought would happen with these guys…so…

Mason hadn't intended to say anything, but found himself agreeing, saying, "I will be their legal custodial guardian as needed-of all five-they are staying together. They will not be separated. I want Mitchell to be able to write checks to pay bills and help his brothers-the boys all need to learn. We can add the others names as it becomes necessary. Mason knew that the boys wanted and needed to stay together. That made sense to Mason. He wouldn't want to lose either of his siblings if he was in their place, but his outburst shocked him as much as anyone else there.

The boys were too young to completely understand the enormity of his outburst, but his wife and the other two men weren't. Was Mandi as shocked as he? She knew Mason did not do anything without studying all the angels first.

The lawyer cut in immediately. He saw an opportunity to help and increase his wage at the same time. "I'll draw up the papers today in that respect and file them, making it legal-o protect everyone, of course," he stated. His thoughts were on his payment as well as all bills being paid and the boys staying together and in their home.

The assistant manager was happy to agree finding this to be a proper way to handle the situation. All three names –Mason's, Mandi's, and Mitchell's- were all added to the new account. The former family account was closed and its funds transferred to the new account. He was ecstatic: he would have a big commission for this.

The lawyer's office was the next stop. Mitchell had many questions about the custodial guardianship as it frightened him a little. The lawyer explained and meant his words to be comforting ones to five young men. "In doing this, Mr. and Mrs. Morgan are assuring all five of you that no one will be able to separate you guys. You can stay together, stay in your home, go to the same school, and continue your life pretty much as you always have. These two adults will simply take over the adult roles in your lives to help you do that." He was assuming the Morgans would just move in and stay on. The lawyer did not know anything personal about the Morgans except what he read in the "Who's Who" in the finance world and he knew they were loaded, loaded, loaded. He intended on charging them at least two hundred dollars an hour today from the time he received the phone call this morning to meet them at the bank until this was finished. Right now he was more than willing to do their bidding. What he did not intend to tell the boys was that the Morgans would also have the right to move the boys with them their home if they so desired. How far they took their role as guardians was not his business. He didn't want to know more than he'd be paid and the boys would be taken care of properly.

He understood that these adults were people of integrity and that their reputations were out-standing.

"I'll have my secretary come in to witness your signatures," Opening the outer door, he beckoned her. "If you and Mrs. Morgan will just sign here, I will get these filed at the courthouse immediately.

Wondering what they were getting into, Mason and Mandi still signed willingly. In less than a day, they felt a bond with these boys already. Mason also easily wrote a check for two thousand dollars and gave it to the lawyer.

"This should cover any paper work and your time for all you have done for these guys," he said. The check was from his personal account, not the new one they had just opened at the bank.

The lawyer looked at the check, his eyes almost popping out, but he managed to control himself and thank them. "Yes, sir, thank you, the best of luck to all of you." He shook hands all around, ushering them out joyously. The man had been generous, the lawyer was happy.

Outside, Mason and Mandi looked at each other, their thoughts on the same wave length. What have we done? And, we were right to do this weren't we? Yes, they both agreed, smiling.

"Anybody hungry?" Mason asked. He was a guy who understood that teens were always, if he and Mandi were taking this seriously, and, yes, they took everything seriously, then they had to take care of the boy's needs both physical and emotional.

Five yeses came out eagerly. "Pizza?" Mandi suggested. Again the yeses were full of expectation.

"Okay, show us where to go, guys. Show us your town's best pizza place," Mason stated.

"There's a great pizza place just around the block. We can walk it from here," Mitch suggested. Mason nodded, "Great, lead the way."

"Does this mean we will be staying here awhile?" Mandi said very quietly to Mason as they walked the block to the pizza parlour.

He nodded, "I do believe it does. We will be busy at the plant for a month at least. I need to check out the workplace and implement some of our plans into action. Are we together on this?" he asked unnecessarily as he held the door open for everyone to enter. Of course, she nodded; he expected as much, as always.

Some customers inside the restaurant greeted the boys, offered their condolences, then eyed the Morgans with open curiosity; neither offered a word of explanation. Mason led them to a table, following a waitress to the back. He let the boys' name their drinks and their pizzas as Mandi ordered a bowl of salad for them. He leaned back in his chair relaxed, waiting for the drinks to appear, and then the salad Mandi had ordered for them all.

The boys were quiet, their minds all on their futures, if even for the rest of the summer.

"Does this guardian thing mean you'll be living with us?" Trenton asked. He was fourteen and would be a freshman in high school next month. He wanted to know if they were trying to take his parent's place. He wasn't too sure how he felt about that. He understood the need to keep them together, knew he should be thankful that they seemed to care enough. He was grateful and thankful, but worried if they cared enough to stay, really stay, and for how long.

"We are not going anywhere. We will be around, yes, Trenton. I need to oversee the transfer of the business ownership and set up a work schedule that Mandi and I agree upon, meet and talk to all the employees, get the business back on track. That's the reason we came here in the first place.

Mandi and I will be around and available for whatever you need, all of you. Don't be embarrassed about asking. Anything at all. Okay? We took the responsibility to help all of you, especially Mitchell. He will need you all to cooperate and work together. So do we. Understand?"

Trenton nodded, a little uneasy, still. Since he was only fourteen, inexperienced, he could only watch and try to trust his brothers and these two adults.

"Ah, here's the pizza. Eat up guys. Enjoy." Mason didn't need to say anymore. Watching them, he could not remember himself ever eating that much. Mandi and Mason each ate three pieces apiece and the others devoured the remains. Salad, too, was gone.

"I'm full," Kyler groaned.

"Me, too," Brendon agreed.

"Me, three," Trenton echoed.

"Then we are ready to leave, I believe," Mason laughed easily. He'd enjoyed watching them, listening to their endless chatter as they ate. He'd never thought he would before. The joy surprised him. He looked at his wife whose face echoed his own feelings. She, too, was mesmerized by these guys. Guys who weren't sure they wanted the adults around one minute, then acted like they'd known them forever the next. Mason shook his head, stood up, put a twenty on the table for a tip, and then went to the counter to pay.

Mitch caught up with him as he was paying. Mason had the new checkbook, he knew. "Don't you want this to come out of that new account, sir?" Mitch asked. To him it was a simple question-paying for their food.

"Oh, no, this is my treat, lad," Mason told him, handing the checker a credit card.

"But…" Mitch began. That money should be there to pay for their food, he thought, not the Morgans.

Mason turned to the teen, casually touched the lad's shoulder as he talked, "I will show you how to set up a spreadsheet for your expenditures and that will include times like this some. Later, okay?"

Mitch nodded. Why he felt so secure with this man around, he didn't understand, but he trusted both of them completely and would let them help him so he could learn from them. Somehow he would get through his senior year. But, he needed this man to show him how. The money would help them live as they always had…together.

In the car Mason brought up another aspect of the boys lives before this past week. Here he'd only known them a day and he was trying to connect the dots, his mind working as usual. "Have you guys ever been to the factory? Did your dad ever take you there?" Mason asked, knowing it was no longer their dad's, but his and Mandi's to run and make profitable.

"None of us have, sir," Kyler spoke up. "Dad said we could work there someday, but that day never came, then he sold it," His voice took on a sad quality, remembering his parents and the why.

"Well, we will have to see about that. I need to do some research, but I'm willing to take anyone there who wants to go; I'm not against you learning. All of you, I mean that," Mason assured them as he drove through town to their quiet neighborhood. The houses were all different sizes, family dwellings where kids played in or near the streets and adults visited as they worked outside, or watched little ones. There was a nice size field to the south side of the Cooke home where many kids gathered to play catch, or run around.

Back at their home, the boys, stomachs full, drifted off to be with others their own age in that field. They were accepting of this new turn of events in their lives, because so far it hadn't prevented them from being themselves or doing what teens do. For now… Mason and Mandi watched as the boys followed what was probably normal routine for them; bounding off in different directions, finding friends. Doing what teens did everywhere.

The teens sidestepped from being in the lawyer's office, learning they would be under the guardianship of these two whom they had just met the day before, to running off to be with friends and forgetting the Morgans were there. Both the Morgans let them go as they had many things to discuss among themselves. They were going to teach five young men to survive, check out the factory they'd just bought a month ago, get that factory on the right track, then they could leave. They knew they needed to be available to Mitchell to help him learn. Available, they would be.

Chapter 2

FRIDAY

Mason and Mandi spent the day at the factory meeting with supervisors, foremen, workers, going over spreadsheets and business tactics. The teens were at home by themselves.

There was plenty of lunch meat for sandwiches and chips and drinks, so they knew the guys could fend for themselves easily. They also had friends near to be around to fill their hours.

Mandi had gone grocery shopping by herself to prevent Mitch from feeling the need for the food she bought to come out of that new account. She and Mason thought the account would be there for the boys when they weren't.

They arrived back at the Cooke home to find the guys outside busy with others playing touch football in the expanse of yard between the two houses, theirs and the nearest neighbor to the south. Mason turned off the RV and watched for a few minutes, smiling and enjoying.

The teens all stopped and studied the RV that pulled into their friends' driveway. If they'd seen the RV before they'd expected it to be gone by now on its way.

"Who's that?"

"The Morgans," Mitch answered. "They are helping us for a while, get financially set up. You know, they are the reason we still have our home to live in and can stay here together, right now. Mitch spoke out honestly because the entire neighborhood knew about their parents and their worries about being alone.

Mitch shook his head. He was Mitch to his friends. His parents had only called him Mitchell when he was in trouble.

"Do we have to quit? Do you have to go?" another friend asked, wondering what this new man and woman were like. Mitch shook his head again. "Let's play," he said waving to Mason and Mandi as they were opening their doors, exiting their vehicles. Mason had a briefcase full of papers and their laptops; lots of work him and Mandi.

She had a couple sacks of groceries. They went inside and set up their laptops, working for an hour or so more until the teens came in talking, complaining of hunger.

Mandi heard them entering and smiled. "Uh oh, I'd better start some supper," she told Mason. She stood and stretched the kinks from being at the laptop. "Do you want me to shut down mine?" she asked Mason.

"No, please," he answered automatically," I'll use it to check some things out and cross reference my figures with yours while you start supper, babe." Mason hadn't taken his eyes or his mind off the screen in front of him as he spoke.

She was used to his preoccupation. As she passed him she reached out to touch him, running her fingers through his neck hairs, leaving them tingling.

"I'm trying to concentrate here, woman," he growled softly. She only laughed, met all five teens, blocking the doorway, watching them interact.

"Do you guys like spaghetti?" she asked, bringing them back to the present.

"Yes, Ma'am," Mitch, told her.

"Yes, Ma'am," Kyler echoed.

She gave them her smile as she suggested they all shower while she prepared the meal, wrinkling her nose teasing them about their odor output.

They laughed as she waved them out of the doorway and each gladly went to shower.

Mandi was a good cook. She and Mason loved good food from normal everyday meals to exotic and tried to create different ones. But, today, Mandi wanted something she was pretty sure all five tens would eat.

Forty minutes later, she sent Trenton in to tell Mason to take a break and come and eat. The dining table was set with spaghetti, sauce, salad, and garlic bread in its center stage. Mandi poured drinks into iced glasses.

"Mmm, delicious, thanks Mrs. Morgan, "Trenton praised her as he served himself a third helping. She only smiled.

"Yes, ma'am, thanks, "Brendon echoed, cleaning his plate and reaching for more after his brother.

You are all welcome; enjoy," she answered.

"She cooked; you guys clean up, please. Mandi, I need you to look at something. I need your opinion," Mason announced. Mason needed Mandi and had decided that the boys could help by cleaning up. Mandi nodded. Together they spent two more hours moving figures around and making adjustments.

Finished with their business, Mason and Mandi then joined the boys in the family room. Both adults were surprised by how much they enjoyed talking to and relating with these boys; boys they had only know a week. The boys talked freely about little things they liked to do. They opened up to Mandi about their parents, how much they missed them, still needed them. Mandi promised to be there for them as long as they needed her to. Mason listened; let Mandi control the conversation. The boys needed a woman's input and Mandi was the one wonderful, special woman in his mind. They ended up talking until it was time for the boys to head straight to bed, as they had already gotten their showers out of the way before dinner.

SATURDAY

"No one should be at the factory today," Mason announced at breakfast. Mandi nodded, knowing he was talking about what they'd decided last night.

"I'll be ready when you are dear," she told him; she knew they would do as they had before at other factories.

"Can we help in anyway?" Mitch asked, wanting them to know how this couple worked together. He wanted to watch and know them better.

Thinking and deciding, Mason nodded; "Sure, Mitchell, if you want to."

"Just Mitch, sir," the lad replied, smiling. Telling him "just Mitch," meant he had accepted Mason totally. His brothers knew this

Mason caught the message of acceptance. "We'll take the car, and then all of you can go, if you want to."

"Great, I do," Aiden announced. The others all nodded.

As they headed there in the car, Mason spelled out what they were trying to do. First they'd tour the plant as Mandi carried a notebook, making notes as they moved about.

Then they went to work physically-some of the stations were rearranged, others eliminated, some combined as they felt necessary. Nothing remained the same as they went from area to area.

Handing Mitch his cell phone, Mason asked him to order pizzas for lunch and they were ready to take a break when they arrived. Mason had also given Mitch two twenties, but found them on the table when they came in to eat.

"I wrote my first check, my treat, "Mitch announced proudly when Mason noticed the money on the table. Mason smiled, understanding; Mitch returned his own smile.

As they ate, they talked about the changes. Mason and Mandi were used to making changes as they acquired new businesses. These guys were new to how businesses profited, how they worked. "Do you think the changes you've made will make a big difference, sir?" Kyler asked as they were eating.

"It should be more efficient this way. We will have to see how the workers react on Monday morning. Some will not be happy with their new jobs; others will easily be accepting. "I don't think I was their favorite person these past few days, so we'll see. They will either do it our way or find a job somewhere else. I'm a stickler there: it's my way or the highway," he quipped, winking at his wife.

"Sir, what will you do if everyone walks out?" Brendon asked, wide eyed. Could that happen?

Mason shrugged, "that hasn't happened as yet, but we'd bring in some of our own people; or move the plant to another location, or just shut down operations, and move something else here. I have many options. You see, we have businesses in almost every state and can afford to do it our way because our way usually triples the profits in a year; from then on, they go up and up."

"Wow," Kyler blew out the word. These two adults sounded really successful. They knew what they wanted from any company they bought and expected it to work. Like he said, all his other companies made profits. So this one would he assumed, right? The boys were all worrying for no really good reason, weren't they? Kyler hoped so. Because, if these two didn't want to make more money, they wouldn't be here, would they? They came here to get this company on its feet, or so they said. "So, if you make that happen, everyone's job will be safe."

When Kyler asked his question as they ate, Mason answered honestly as always. "Yes, Kyler, I do. Mandi and I are not new at this. We know what works, what doesn't. Modifications are always needed because people are different. But, this will work; our names are at stake here."

"Are you really rich, Mr. Morgan?" Aiden asked.

Shrugging, Mason answered, "Yes, Aiden, we're billionaires at last count, but money is not the most important thing in the world. Doing my job right is my goal. I really want all the workers to understand that."

"If it didn't work, that would mean a lot of people out of work, Mitch said. "Would that go against our dad? Some of our friends' parents work there."

That thought had never occurred to Mason. Leave it to the teen to come up with that side of the coin. Mason was honest. "It really shouldn't affect him or you guys in any way because this will work. I want to make this business triple its profits within the next year. I want it to succeed," Mason admitted to Mitch and the others." That's the only outcome I'll accept. I will succeed; we will succeed, so therefore, this plant will begin to flourish. Ask Mandi, that's how we operate." He winked at his wife; the teens looked from him to her.

She smiled and added, "If the plant triples, there are always bonuses for the workers. We benefit, they benefit; that's only fair."

"Let's clean up here and finish our job," Mason suggested, as the food was gone.

"Mandi spoke up; changing the subject to one she had mentioned to her husband earlier, "Mason, did you look at the size of that cloak room? If that were removed, this room would be big enough."

He knew what she was suggesting and nodded. "It might work; it has in other places. We'll mention it Monday morning at our meeting and take a count." Mason was open to her plans as well as his own, as they were usually insightful and productive.

"What are they talking about?" Kyler whispered to Mitch as they tool the pizza boxes outside to a dumpster.

"You got me, Kyler, but we can ask them. They said we could ask them anything, didn't they?" Mitch said to his brother in a normal tone as they were outside by then. They finished cleaning up the break room and went in search of their brothers and their guardians. They found them in the reception area rearranging the furniture as they talked.

"I want this desk over there," Mason said as he carried the oak chair to another wall. Two of the boys followed him with the desk. "Thanks," he told "them.

"And, I want to move these chairs to the opposite wall to open up the room," Mandi said as she lifted one side of a chair; Trenton carried the other side.

The boys were having fun pitching in, helping them with the reorganization at the plant. They were feeling like they were really a part of a new beginning that they could see developing. They also hoped that these changes worked okay, because as they said, some of their friends' parents were employees here. They had investments in seeing it succeed, for many different reasons.

"Thanks," Mason said to the boys as they all piled into the car around four o'clock that evening. "You saved us a lot of time and sore muscles helping.

"Speak for yourself, jock," Mandi quipped. "My legs are complaining already. This vacation is hard on me. Maybe we need to go home, back to our plush offices and plusher chairs and spas." He knew she didn't mean it because of satisfied smile, but the boys didn't. Listening to Mandi, they found a need to worry. Did she really mean she wanted to leave? But she had worked so hard at the factory; that was part of her job, wasn't it? They hadn't done anything wrong-they had tried to help. So, why would she want to leave? Was she just tired? They were.

"Hmm," Mason returned, a twinkle in his eyes;" next you're going to tell me I'm cooking tonight, "aren't you?" He gave her a sly smile, wiggling his eyebrows. She laughed; she was the only one to see his expression. She nodded.

Mason changed the subject because he wanted the answer to why they had come here; why they had left their plush offices. Mandi was the reason. Normally they flew to the new locations if they couldn't take care of everything on their computers. "Dear, have I satisfied those two things you wanted on this vacation?" he teased.

"In spades, love, you are my prince. I love you," she told him, not caring that they weren't alone.

Curious glances passed among those listening along with shrugged shoulders and raised eyebrows. No one elaborated, no one asked; they did smile at each other. They were not used to these adults and how they communicated with each other. They had been sure that their parents loved each other, although they very seldom heard them profess that love openly in front of them.

Mason hit the blinker and pulled into a grocery store parking lot. "I shall return, relax, my love," he told his wife, and then nodded when Kyler opened his door to get out. Mitch, Trenton, and Brendon also joined him leaving Aiden in the car with Mandi. Aiden was tired, too, and scrunched down in the seat, closing his eyes, letting the others do the shopping.

Hamburgers, hot dogs, buns for both, chips, pop, can beans, potato salad, brownies-Mason loaded all these items into a cart he was pushing.

As they walked, to Mitch he said, "I saw that grill out back. Is it charcoal or propane?" The guys were wise; they knew they would be eating out on the grill tonight.

"Propane, sir, and it's full, I know," Mitch told him.

"Great! Then, we are lighting it tonight. I think we have enough.... What, Trenton?...Yes, that's fine," he said to a bag of cookies that Trenton had picked up.

Mason paid for the food without Mitch or the others commenting on his doing so, then headed home to light the grill. The boys loved eating this way and enjoyed helping. They knew where the outdoor tools were for the grill, where the tablecloth was for the picnic table and the trays for things out and in as needed.

Mandi sat in a lounge chair after her long hot shower and watched. The boys did not give a thought to how they were interacting with Mason, but both he and Mandi both felt the connection. Mandi listened as Mason talked as he welded the spatula, sharing some of his past with these guys.

"Sometimes, we do this to inspire attendance and productivity at some of our factories; whenever they would reach their goals and had perfect attendance, Mandi and I would provide food for all the workers and their families at a park. We find it helps. At first the crowd would be small, but as the word leaked out to the fellow workers, the crowds grew. Soon every member of those factories was in perfect attendance at work and at the cookouts. The plant managers take over the cookouts, and the workers get to know each other. It breeds a better work environment. Maybe that will encourage attendance and improve production here along with our changes."

Mason looked at Mandi, "What do you think, love?"

Mandi smiled and did a twisting motion with her hands. She'd think about it, he knew.

The guys had helped make the hamburger patties, provided Mason with the tools, and cleaned off the picnic table. They brought out the condiments, the utensils, plates, and glasses filled with ice for their pop. Someone watching them would not have known they were two separate entities-they talked, ate, laughed, played catch with a football, even. They were happy, these teens, but in the back of their minds were Mandi's words about going back to their plush offices. How could they make her, them want to stay? Was this their goal, what these guys really wanted? They knew they had to decide soon before the Morgans said they were leaving. The longer the Morgans stayed with the teens, the more settled the teens would feel. The Morgans believed this and felt the teens would be okay on their own with their guidance. The teens were beginning to feel that they didn't want the Morgans to leave, ever. But they were afraid to commit to the idea of permanency. They liked the Morgans more every day and hoped that the Morgans liked the Cooke young men enough to stick it out a little while longer.

During their conversation this evening, the Cooke teens found out that Mason had gone to college on a full football scholarship and still loved the game. Mitch loved the game, as did his brothers.

Mandi was the brains of their operations, Mason told the boys during their dinner. She was truly good at accessing problems and finding the correct solution. Together they were successful, he admitted. The boys took turns firing questions at Mason, asking about their personal lives and habits, getting to know these adults. They needed to know if they wanted them to stay, and how to do that if they did.

The Morgans had been married for ten years now. No, they didn't have any children of their own. It just hadn't happened. They'd been so busy building their company; they hadn't taken time to find out why. Yes, they both liked children and had wanted them when they thought about it. Maybe they still would. Mason told them.

"But, you do like kids, right?" Trenton asked. They had to or else they wouldn't still be here trying to help them, he thought.

"Of course," Mason answered. They were still sitting around the table eating the cookies Trenton had chosen.

"We love children," Mandi added. "That's why I want to turn that huge break room into a daycare for the working moms. It would increase attendance, reduce absentees." She knew they had tried this before and found success

"A daycare?" Kyler questioned, "Where? "

"Because, dear, it really helps parents, especially single moms, when schools have half days and breaks as most of these cannot afford the extra day care expense, she answered.

Kyler liked hearing her call him "dear," it made him feel close to her, even though he thought it might be a slip of her tongue, or something she always said. He still liked it.

"Was your mom a working mom?" Aiden asked, wisely thinking she knew what she was talking about.

Mandi nodded, 'Yes, she was. From the tine I was ten, I was home alone on those days behind locked doors with only myself for company. It was lonely as I couldn't call or talk or play with any of my friends. So, I kept a journal and I've used some of those ideas in our business. Experience helps."

"So, you benefited in one way," Trenton spoke up. She nodded.

"Our mom never worked. She was always here," Brendon added.

Mandi smiled. She really liked these boys, more every day. She was sure her husband felt the same way. The more they were around them, the more they would find it harder to leave.

"I benefited because I'm a dreamer and I found a way to make my dreams realities. I worked hard to get my education. I went to college on scholarships like many others. I worked toward my goal, met Mason, and found out we had the same ideas, the same goals. We worked together to achieve our goals; make our lives what they are now. I couldn't have done it without Mason, he completed me. Lucky for us we met at college and connected." She looked across the table at her mate, her eyes full of the love they shared. His eyes mirrored hers.

"Was it love at first sight for you two? Mom said she loved dad after their first date," Kyler said.

No, not at all," Mandi admitted, hiding her smile, barely. Mason burst out laughing.

"Go ahead, tell them," Mason said between bouts of laughter. He repeated, "Go ahead, and tell them how you never dreamed an overachieving football star who was the valedictorian of his class would ever look at a cute skinny freshman before the year was over. Let alone, fall in love with her before she graduated- tell them-because we were so much alike after all. Tell them your side, my dear."

Mandi rolled her eyes at his tale, and then proceeded to tell them her side anyway. They had asked her side after all. "I thought he was a conceded jock and I told him that being the star quarterback meant nothing to me. I made him prove his worthiness." She was grinning.

"She shot me down," Mason shook his head as he said this, then added, "at first."

Mitch caught the part that was important to him. "You were the star quarterback in college?" Mitch was duly impressed; he loved football. Mason shrugged, but Mitch wanted more. "Would you, could you teach me some techniques... about football. I'm not a star or a quarterback, but I love to play? If I get good enough, maybe I can get a scholarship to collage." Mitch didn't want to think that losing their parents meant none of them were going to college. Mitch looked at Mason in a different light now. He wasn't just a successful business man now, who cared enough to help them out; he'd been the star quarterback at his college. That was important. And, the college was a big one, well known. Most important, he had befriended them. He really cared, Mitch was sure of this.

Mason cared more than he'd even admitted to himself, or to Mandi, yet. How was he going to just walk away from these guys, especially Mitch, whom he'd grown very fond of in just a few days? "I'd be glad to, Mitch, tomorrow, anytime we're free, Mason told the boy he loved. Loved? As a son? Yes, he did. The realization hit Mason like a hammer, knocking him senseless. But then he looked at this young man and his heart swelled: with joy, with happiness. Wow! He loved this seventeen-year-old as a son-like a father. He was stunned. It took a minute for him to recover. He changed the subject.

"I cooked. I get to go take my shower," Mason announced, rising, stretching. Not forgetting that they weren't alone, not caring anymore because he'd gotten to know these five siblings, Mason walked around the picnic table, bent down and kissed Mandi in front of them all. It wasn't just a peck, either; it was enough to leave her wanting more. Although it was too short for her liking it did promise her something more sensual to follow.

She could wait. She licked her lips when he drew back, tasting milk and cookies, and his hamburger. "Go shower, jock," she teased.

He left them, with a silly grin on his face and rushed his shower. Mason loved Mandi with his whole soul. She was his. He was hers .Forever wasn't long enough. Now, the realization that he loved Mitch and maybe the other four had him floating. He and Mandi had been honest and open with these boys, found them being honest and open in return, and accepting. And, they'd fallen head first into a family. He and Mandi had always said they wanted a family. Now, they had a ready-made one, a family to be proud of, that was, of course, if the boys wanted them to stay and be a family.

He hadn't been alone much with Mandi since coming here, wondered if being here would cause a wedge between them. But, no, when he had kissed her, he'd felt like a teenager again, as usual. He couldn't wait to be alone with her-contemplated it as left to shower. How early would the boys go to bed? Could they go to bed and leave the boys to fend for themselves? Their going first would surely tell the boys their intentions, wouldn't it? Was that a bad thing? These guys were capable of understanding their needs, weren't they? Oh, what did he know!

Mandi watched Mason leave, all the way into the house. "Aiden, why don't you go on up and take your shower," Mandi suggested that he follow

Mason. "Then we can all watch a movie after everyone's showered. I'll even pop popcorn," she enticed.

Achy and tired, Aiden didn't need any prodding, agreed easily, followed by his brothers after they helped with the cleanup, until all six males were freshly showered, camped out on the rec room furniture, discussing what movie they wanted to watch.

A little louder than necessary, Mason said, "as long as you don't let Mandi choose the movie, we will be okay," as Mandi entered with huge bowls of popcorn.

Hey, jock, I heard that," she teased passing out the bowls.

"That's why he said it," Brendon told her grinning.

"Oh," she said with raised eyebrows, pretending she didn't already know that. Mason caught on as had she, they were enjoying the foreplay.

Everyone had popcorn but Mason who rose, grabbed her, picked her up, and carried her to the chair he'd been sitting in. He settled back down with her on his lap. "Who needs popcorn," he whispered to her as he nibbled her ear and neck. He caught Kyler and Trenton watching, funny looks on their faces. "Your parents never kissed in front of you?" he asked.

"Not like that," Kyler admitted, ducking his head, blushing.

"I thought that stuff was for newlyweds or on TV only," Trenton said. He, too, was a little embarrassed, but curious.

"We are," Mason said his arms still around Mandi. She was relaxed in her cuddled position on his lap. She'd been there many times thoroughly enjoyed it.

"You told us you have been married ten years," Brendon reminded him. He was also curious.

"Oh then, we're still teenagers at heart, right, love?" Mason was full of comebacks. Mandi made no comment.

Brendon rolled his eyes, turned around to the TV, the movie, his popcorn.

The showers and the movie did the trick. Five teens headed to bed afterwards, the physical act of activity having worn them out. Mandi had kept her position on Mason's lap, snuggled down, only half watching the movie. "Don't go to sleep on me girl" Mason whispered. She smiled, wanting what he was promising with his teasing kisses during the whole movie.

SUNDAY

"Where do you go to church?" Mandi asked as the table filled with teens, intent on filling their hungry stomachs. She was assuming they went to church weekly. Did they? They would now, she thought.

"A couple blocks away, there's a church mom and dad always took us to." Kyler answered. It was where the funeral had been he remembered, sadly.

"Then that's where we will go today. Tell me how you like your eggs, so we can eat before we go," she offered.

"Scramble a dozen of them and that'll do," Mitch told her.

She eyed him "Only a dozen?" she teased. She scrambled eighteen and they were devoured. Funny how they were hungry again soon after church was over. So they ate an early lunch.

Mitch dug out the football after lunch and tossed it to Mason who smiled, catching it. They all knew they'd take the game outside. No one wanted to be left out as all five teens followed Mason outside. For him alone, Mandi whispered as he passed her, "there goes your heart." What man could resist tossing a ball around with a kid? Mason couldn't, no way, no how, that was for sure.

"Rolling his eyes, he told her, "I'm afraid it's already gone, love."

"Mine, too," she agreed. After cleaning up the kitchen, she found a lawn chair and settled down to watch the guys. Neighborhood kids soon filtered out and joined them.

Mitch proudly told his friends: "he was the star quarterback at his college."

"Wow!" one kid said, "What college?"

"Yeah, what college did you go to?" another one asked Mason.

Mason was not above telling them about his alma mater. He had enjoyed his time there. "Southern Cal." Mason informed them.

"That's a pretty big College," Mitch said with pride in his voice for his new friend. Hero worship was too small; he was enthralled and happy about it He had someone to brag about.

Mandi used her cell phone to order food for their supper as she watched. She had eight large pizzas delivered for the whole group as no one seemed to think of supper; they were too into the game. Not even the other boys who had joined them wanted to stop. They all ate. They played until it was too dark to play.

In just five days Mason and Mandi had met and fallen deeply in love with five young men. What were they going to do?

MONDAY

Leaving all five at home on Monday to fend for themselves was what they had to do to take care of business, but there was plenty of food and beverages, and friends to entertain them. They weren't that young, Mandi had to tell herself. They let the boys sleep in; as usual, Mason and Mandi were up at six, ate breakfast, and planned their day at the factory.

Mandi made cinnamon rolls from a can, actually five cans, and there was milk and juice ready for when they did wake. She left them a note: we are at the factory. That number is 462-5912; our cell numbers are 555-1091 and 555-1743 if you need us for anything. We should be home around four. Cinnamon rolls are in the oven. Have a good day, see you later. She signed her name, but made herself leave out the word "love" although she really wanted to right that word. "Mrs. M" was enough for now.

Mason and Mandi stood in front of all the workers; Mason began his speech. "Good morning everyone. We met most of you last week. Some of you are new faces. We are the new owners, my wife and I, and take my word for it right now-from the start, her word and ideas are as important as mine. We are a team.

"Now-all of you are wondering what happened to your plant over the weekend. We happened. We are the owners and we want to see this plant make a profit. That's what business is all about. We ..."

Mandi took her cue, she spoke up. "We have moved things around and when we are through explaining how this new plant will be run, we will expect your complete cooperation. There will be incentives for meeting your quotas. There will be bonuses, too, especially for workmanship and attendance. All of these will be taken into attendance. It was Mandi's turn to pause and let Mason have another turn.

"My wife has decided that maybe a day care would help attendance. Could I see a show of hands if you are interested in seeing this incorporated into this building, at no cost to you, of course. Mason paused as he and Mandi tried to count the hands that were raised compared to the workers in attendance. It seemed good.

"We will discuss this with you, later."

"Okay, next-you can see the changes we've made. If you'll find what you think is your station, we will both come around and explain the changes. There were some stations eliminated; you were not eliminated, we will simply reposition you. Let's get to work."

Mason and Mandi were very busy the whole day. They walked around,, explaining what they wanted, talking, meeting employees, moving people where they thought worked better for the workers. They were patient and friendly at all times, taking stock of peoples' attitudes and the situations. Everyone worked. They were trying, cooperating. It seemed they all wanted to protect their jobs. This knowledge made the Morgans happy. A company buy-out did not have to mean loss of jobs for anyone. Keeping everyone on the payroll was the best solution.

Shift managers were trained to run certain machines so when someone needed a break, these machines were not shut down. Break times and bathroom breaks were discussed. No shift manager was allowed to just sit and observe. They were expected to work along with the other workers, keeping the lines running smooth and constant. This was something new for the shift managers; they were used to being supervisors who walked around and mainly watched. If Mason stopped walking to run a machine to demonstrate how it could be, then he would expect the shift managers to be willing to do the same. They were not better or more important than the workers; they were there to keep the line moving freely and smoothly. For eight hours every day, from seven in the morning until three-thirty in the afternoon.

At quitting time, Mason took a minute to express his thanks, "I wish to thank all of you for your progress today. When this business turns a profit, you will enjoy some of those profits. You will not just be padding our pockets; you will be padding your own. Thank you, have a good evening. See you tomorrow."

Chapter 3

Two weeks later

Mason addressed the workers; "I just want five minutes of your time before work begins. Is everyone clocked in? I always pay you to listen to me." He paused, smiled, continued, "these past two weeks have been excellent. I want to personally thank you." He turned to his wife, "Mandi."

Mandi stepped up to the microphone. "I have reviewed everyone's progress and willingness to go along with our changes. And that willingness will not go unrewarded. I'm implementing a raise, a small one today, but it's a promise of more. Good day." She put the microphone down. The murmuring about the raise information was immediate. Everyone was excited.

Mason said, "Have a good day, ladies and gentleman. We will be in our office adjusting the new pay scales to reflect the raises starting today."

Two weeks had gone by at work and at the Cooke home. Mason was true to his word to Mitch, setting up a spread sheet for the household bills. When the power bill came, he let Mitch write a check to pay it. The same was true for the garbage bill and the water bill.

"The food is my responsibility since we are living here too," he told Mitch, who tried to argue that there were five of them and only he and Mandi. But, Mason explained, "We are also using the electricity and water, do you want me to divide them too?" Mitch had shaken his head. "Then don't complain about how I want to contribute, Mitch, just learn how to do this part for now. Now this is your new balance," Mason said. "And, you know when these bills come and when they are due. We'll add up what you need for next month when we sit down again. Just relax. You will catch on."

Mitch was worried. He had to make sure he and his brothers had everything that they needed and that the money stretched until Aiden was out of school. Five years, hopefully the money would last.

Mason was patient and Mitch appreciated that. Mitch thought Mason was paying too much out of his own pocket to save their money for when the Morgans had to leave and he and his brothers would be on their own.

School would start in a few weeks and there would be many more expenses, Mitch was afraid. He and his brothers would have to learn to live frugally.

"Thanks so much for being patient with me, Mr. Morgan," Mitch said. He wanted this man to know how much it really meant to him.

"No problem at all. Mitch; I'm happy to help," Mason said sincerely.

Mitch looked up to Mason who had worked hard to get his own education, and then to build up a business with his wife. He was still too young to know that his hero worship was also embedded in trust and a love that was growing inside him. There were times when Mitch would just watch how Mason interacted with him and his brothers, and then tell himself that he had only known this man a month or so. Mitch had a special place in Mason's heart, yet Mason knew he cared deeply for the other four young men; he just hadn't voiced this out loud.

After the boys retired to bed each night, the two adults shared their feelings. Both were surprised and ecstatic that, not only did they both admit to falling deeply for these five teens but they also dreaded losing them out of their lives.

SATURDAY

"Good morning, guys," Mandi greeted each of them cheerfully as they trouped in, smelling her cooking, led around by their noses. "We have plans today," Mandi started with, but was interrupted.

"You have to work today?" Kyler asked, his features drooping. They had all missed these two adults in their lives during the past two weeks while they were working. Even though they'd been busy with friends, they wanted the security of the Morgans.

Mandi reached out, and touched Kyler's mouth to still his comment, surprising him into silence. No one had ever done it that way before: just the touch. He didn't understand that it also touched his heart.

Mandi continued, "I was going to say, Kyler, that school will be starting again and I want to know what you need. Clothes, shoes, and supplies, whatever you need-I want to know now. We are new at this, so we need your cooperation. If each of you will make us a list, I want to address those lists today, after breakfast.

They all sat down to await her feeding them with food she usually prepared every morning, a little confused by her request. Instead, she handed each one a slip of paper and a pen. They glanced at each other. They looked at Mandi, then at Mason for help.

"Make your lists: socks, shoes, jeans, what do you need before school starts?" she said as she opened the refrigerator.

As she was pouring glasses of milk and juice to go with the pancakes she had warming in the oven, Mitch spoke up, "We will be okay: you don't have to do this."

Smiling to soften her words, she said, "Don't contradict me: Mitch, make your list.

He returned her smile, said, "yes, ma'am." They could only do as she asked. He and his brothers all followed her suggestion and made their lists while they ate their breakfast.

Mason watched their faces as he ate, smiling to himself.

Mitch looked over at Mason and saw something he thought was gone forever, that he'd never see again: a father's love. Does he really love us? Mitch thought so. In less than a month Mason wasn't a stranger any longer. In those four weeks he had become very important to Mitch. To all of them, Mitch was sure. Was that why none of them could ever call the Morgans by their first names when they talked? Mitch wondered. It just seemed so wrong, disrespectful. Mr. Morgan had stepped in and stepped up to the plate. He hadn't tried to replace their father, but had become an important father figure in a short time.

And, Mrs. Morgan, she was always there for whatever they needed, like now. She filled her role as a mother without being pushy in any way-except now, maybe, but Mitch liked how she took over because he could tell she cared.

Mason smiled at Mitch and watched the lad as proud as any real father could be. Mitch nodded at Mason and looked down at his list. They usually all got new shoes to start in and new jeans, as he'd usually outgrown his, while the three younger ones got the hand-me-downs. Kyler's legs were as long as his so he got more new jeans, too. Mitch thought that if his list were short, she wouldn't spend too much money. Was that the right way to think? Mitch worried.

Mitch took a peak at Mandi who'd sat down on his left. Yeah, she, too, had won his heart. Cooking, cleaning, doing their laundry, all the while, she worked forty hours a week at the factory with her husband. Yes, she had enlisted them to do their part as their own parents had before, but she had been right there for them, Always.

"Are we going right after we finish breakfast? He asked her when she looked at him and smiled.

"Yes, Mitch, we are. Your list looks short," she noted. She understood how Mitch worried about any money that she and Mason spent on them, but they were enjoying it, so she intended to do what she could, and Mitch was just going to have to accept it.

"Yes. Ma'am, I don't need much, a couple pair of jeans, maybe a pair of shoes, that's all, really. My jeans and Kyler's, since his legs are as long as mine, get passed down to the others. See, we really don't need much, honest."

"You don't wear shorts to school to start…because of the weather?" she asked, tilting her head toward him as she spoke.

Mitch answered, "Yes, we do, but we don't need shorts. Honest. We have plenty," Mitch didn't want to put too much on her or her husband.

Mandi let his comments slide for now. She knew by the amount of clothes she'd seen them wear that they had never done without-she had laundered them. She and Mason had talked about this day; they wanted to do this. It might be their only opportunity. Neither was sure how much longer they would be here. Both thought that when the boys went back to school and were in their regular routines, they would no longer be needed. It would be time to say, "Goodbye." No, neither of them was ready to say "Goodbye." Neither of them wanted to leave, but they would do what was right for these boys-even if it meant leaving them, losing them. Both adults had admitted to each other how attached they had become to all five boys for at least five times the reasons. So, today was a special day, a farewell gift to these boys.

Taking their mother's van, they made the shoe store their first stop. Everyone chose a different style of shoes to suit their tastes. Mitch started to argue with Mason about paying-quietly-he didn't want to be embarrassing in front of the clerk who didn't know them. But, Mitch also didn't want Mason using his money when they had money.

The sale clerk didn't understand why Mitch was interrupting his father during the transaction, unless he'd changed his mind about his own choice. The clerk just assumed that they were a family because they interacted as a unit.

Mason turned to Mitch and whispered, "Back off. I'm doing this." Mitch could tell he meant the words. Actually, he was a bit upset by Mason's comment, so he murmured:" Sorry," as he stepped back. His eyes stayed on the cash register as the total was rung up. It was almost five hundred dollars. Did their parents spend that much every time? Mitch new they each always chose the style they wanted without their parents balking, so it had to be true. Truly this was too much for the Morgans to spend on someone else's kids, Mitch thought. Or, did Mason feel the closeness that Mitch was feeling? Was he doing this because of how much he cared? Mitch thought that he'd seen this caring closeness this morning in Mason's eyes. Mitch hoped that the Morgans were not just doing this out of some responsibility thing. He hoped it was a sign of love. A sign that they loved him and his brothers!

Mandi stepped up behind Mitch, touched his arm to get his attention, whispered, "Let us do this as a present for you and your brothers. We want to, please."

He smiled, nodded, relaxed. They wanted to do this. It wasn't just a responsibility. He heard her caring words and they comforted him. Mitch stepped to her side and felt her love envelope him. He was seventeen and considered himself almost grown, but he understood how much he needed and wanted to still be a kid sometimes, letting someone else take control. He was willing to give that control over to her and her husband.

So, at the clothing store where they usually bought their jeans, each boy picked out two pair. She made them try them on and no one complained at this. Mandi understood about jeans being passed down as one outgrew them, so the three younger ones did not need more than two new pair. They had shorts to start out with and enough jeans to do throughout the week. But Mitch had mentioned that his and Kyler's legs were the same length, so both of them would need more than two new pair of new jeans. Kyler was as tall as Mitch already with Brendon not far behind.

"How many days of week do you go to school?" Mandi asked Kyler.

"Five," he admitted, sheepishly.

"Then how many pairs of jeans do you and Mitch need each?" she asked, holding back a smile, her eyes on Kyler's face alone.

"We don't," Mitch started. There came her hand up again, gently touching his lips to quiet him this time. It worked. Mitch took a breath and went quiet, watching her. Her eyes remained on Kyler, waiting. Kyler was embarrassed.

"Do you want me to choose the styles you wear," she asked Kyler. He shook his head. He'd never liked his mom's choices. Could hers be any different? "Then do it," she advised, "both of you." They did.

When Mandi noticed Brendon was having trouble deciding on two out of three pairs he liked, she took and put all three pairs into the cart, giving Brendon a hand motion and a look. He didn't argue, even though he thought about it.

She turned to the other three and told them to look at shirts. All five were kept busy until she was satisfied.

"Can't you control her?" Mitch asked of Mason, half teasing, half embarrassed by Mandi's actions.

Mason grinned. He'd followed them around letting Mandi control the shopping here without commenting. "I value my life too much," he retorted, smiling, "Besides, I'm in total agreement with her," he added. Mitch groaned, Mason laughed and gave Mitch a quick hug across the shoulders. It was just a touch, but both males were affected beyond words.

Shopping, a quick lunch, more shopping, and then some grocery shopping on top of that: all the males were ready to groan loudly until Mandi announced, "Let's go home," and made them feel better.

When all the new clothes and the groceries were put away, the boys went outside to avoid any more requests from her. Did they really mind? No, they were happy.

Mason had joined Mandi in the kitchen putting away the groceries. As they worked, they talked, as usual. The love they had found here was more than any they could believe existed. They both loved Mason's nieces and nephews but found this experience so enlightening and overwhelming. Finished with that chore, Mason had a request, "Can I do what I want, now?" Mandi slipped her arms around his waist and stepped as close as she could, looking up at him.

"What do you have in mind, love?"

He leaned down and whispered, "This. Let's go out and make sure the RV's still okay." He raised his eyebrows, wigged them.

"Hmm, that sounds tempting."

They didn't pull apart when two of the teens entered the kitchen at that moment heading for the refrigerator for drinks.

"Guess I have to take a rain check on that one…but back to my first thought before you railroaded me." She smiled up at him, him alone. They were not paying any attention to the teens.

"What do you want, love?"

"I think I've been replaced," he teased, glancing at the boys.

"Never," she breathed out.

"I want to talk to you about something important," he returned.

"Really."

"Yes, ma'am, really important." He was grinning. Mason was used to the tit-for-tat with his wife. They both enjoyed teasing each other; it kept life from being boring; but he really had been thinking ahead to the next month when the boys went to school. If they were still here and he knew they both wanted to be, then his idea was very important. It would benefit all of them. Mason liked thinking of them together as a unit. It was comforting.

Until now, all of their business endeavors had taken the place of any family they hadn't had. Until now, they had been very satisfied with their life, or so Mason had thought until Mandi suggested this trip. Until now, Mason hadn't known anything was missing. He hadn't known he needed more. He was happy. Now, he knew true happiness, having found these five siblings to be a part of his life-of their lives. He needed to thank Mandi for giving him this opportunity to grow. To love. To live.

"I believe we need another car here. With school starting the boys will need one and we cannot drive the RV all aver." There…he'd succeeded in changing the subject back to his original one, a necessity.

She was calm. "Okay, I'll agree to that, dear. What are we going to buy?"

They were on the path to becoming even more deeply involved in life here in this town and they were embracing it with fervor

"I haven't looked yet. I'd like your opinion. He looked at the two teens that had stayed in the room, drinking, nosy. Trenton and Brendon were not trying to hide their interest in watching the adults at play. Mason eyed them over Mandi's head, and said, "Go get your brothers. You might as well come too. Really," he prodded. "I mean it. Move."

Grinning at all they had seen and heard, excited at the prospect of car shopping, these two brothers sat down their glasses and went for their brothers. Soon all seven were at a car dealership, walking around, and all trying to tell Mason what he needed. Mitch and Kyler wanted Mason to choose a sporty one that they could borrow later on…maybe. They didn't think of the permanency of this thought. Did they realize that would mean the Morgans were staying? Not on the surface…yet, but the seeds were being planted. Mason saw right through their 'suggestions' and vetoed them, smiling.

"Ah, come on," Kyler teased-Mason popped him on the back of the head and laughed.

"How many people will be riding in this vehicle?" Mason asked calmly. He and Mandi chose a three seated minivan that had room for all of them, one that Mandi herself approved of as she would be doing most of the driving, Mason believed. He watched their sighs register their desire for a smaller four seater, a Pontiac Grand Prix that was a little sporty, but still reasonable. The guys were pleased with it, he could tell.

He named a price to the dealer for both vehicles, knowing what he was asking. "Give me this deal and I'll take both vehicles," Mason told the salesman who haggled and figured, and then agreed to Mason's quote. The salesman still made a good percentage selling both cars. Mason wrote a check covering the total cost of the cars in full, shocking the salesman. A quick call to Mason's bank accountant guaranteed the funds and the paperwork was finished. Three cars could drive off the lot that afternoon.

Mason surprised Mitch by handing the keys to the smaller car to him. Mitch's eyes were saucers. "You do know the way home? You won't get lost?" Mason teased.

Mitch recovered. "The long way or the short way?" he asked, grinning.

"Don't push your luck, "Mason returned, ruffling up the boy's hair. Mitch laughed, clearly enjoying the joke, while he ran his fingers through his hair to repair it to its disarray.

Eagerly, Kyler asked, "Can I ride with Mitch?"

"Me, too, please?" Brendon added.

"Please!" Kyler begged.

Mason nodded to them, then added, "Behave, all three of you, and go straight home." He and Mandi watched the three teens pile into the new car, smiling as they drove away. Then they each drove the minivans home and into the garage, leaving the smaller car outside under an overhang.

"It drives so different," Mitch told Mason, excitedly as he handed over the keys. He was only used to minivans.

MONDAY

NINE DAYS LATER

"Ready, guys, let's go," Mason hurried the four older guys along. Mandi would be with Aiden getting him registered at the junior high school while he took the other four to the high school for their registration.

Aiden watched the newer minivan back out of the driveway with his brothers and Mason. He was alone with Mandi in the sportier car-cool. But, he was feeling awkward. None of his friends had met Mandi and he wasn't sure how to introduce her. She was his guardian, he understood that, but how do you say that to someone. "This is my guardian," sounded strange to Aiden. She was so much more to him and he wanted to convey that to her and his friends and the teachers, too. So, Aiden was quiet, except for giving her directions to the junior high school where he'd be an eighth grader. All of his brothers were now in high school, leaving him behind for the first time.

At school, Aiden slowly led the way to the office where they met with the principle, filled out papers stating she, and her husband, was his legal guardian. She had a copy for them to photocopy for their records .She paid his tuition for the year and for a month's worth of school lunches. She accompanied him to his home room where she met his teacher there, again explaining that she and her husband were his legal guardians. She left him there for the pep talk about what was expected from the students for a good year. She went out to the car to wait.

Her cell phone kept her busy as she made a few business calls to check on other places they owned. She took care of what she could while she waited. The California office was full of information that she told them to forward to her laptop.

"How'd it go?" she asked Aiden, smiling at him as he approached the car.

He shrugged. "It's school. It's okay, I guess." He was noncommittal.

"Aiden."

"Yes. Ma'am."

"I want what's best for you. That includes an education. Make the best of it, okay?" She started the car. He nodded, gave her a half smile.

"Let's go meet your brothers and have lunch." He smiled more broadly and said, "Okay." She let him direct her from the junior high to the high school.

Mason drove to the high school following Mitch's directions with the four older boys. They were all talking, excited about seeing some of their friends again, and about Mason, too. The boys were proud to show off their guardian; they thought he was cool. Mason, on the other hand was nervous as he parked and turned the car off. They were the ones getting registered for school, but he was a wreck. If he could face down opponents in a board room or new employees in a take-over or buy out, he couldn't he? He could get all four of these guys registered for high school.

"Who's first?" he asked, opening his door, pocketing his keys.

"Trenton, freshman," his brother Brendon teased.

"And, you'll have his back when he needs you, right?" Mason mentioned.

"Yes, sir," Brendon answered, sheepish.

Mason said no more on that. "Come on. You know we should stop by the office first and get that part out of the way. He patted his breast pocket; then peaked inside to make sure he had a copy of the guardianship papers. "Let's go. Show me the way."

At the office the staff was surprised. No one believed the boys would be together. They had speculated on how the boys would manage their future, separated, if they would all return to this school together even. No one had given a thought to someone taking on the responsibility of all five of them, keeping them all together.

Everything was in order, so the principal directed the boys to their respective home rooms to complete the orientation. Soon their guardian would join them, after signing paper after paper, and receiving copies of the handbook plus other information about the school with its extracurricular activity schedule. She then had a student escort Mason to the freshman homeroom where he found out Trenton hadn't had a physical yet and needed that before the first month was over.

"Did you know this?" he asked Trenton when the lad handed him the form for the doctor. "Why didn't you tell us, Trenton?" Mason spoke very quietly for Trenton's ears only.

Trenton was unsure how to answer. "Sorry," he replied, "I guess I forgot because of all that happened this summer." Trenton apologized. "I'm ready to go, sir." Mason wrote out a check for books and one for school lunches, handed the two checks to Trenton to give his home room teacher. The teacher wanted the boy to introduce Mason to him; the teacher, like others in town, knew that the boy's parents had passed away and wanted to know and meet the person responsible for the Cooke teens.

They repeated the same procedure as he and Trenton found Brendon's room. Mason wrote two more checks and introduced himself to Brendon's home room teacher. Then, they went on to Kyler's homeroom for the writing of two more checks and the introduction to that teacher. Finally the four males arrived at Mitch's homeroom.

"I'm glad that's over," Kyler admitted as they reached Mitch's room. Mitch was busy talking to a group of friends. 'Want me to hurry Mitch up?" Kyler asked Mason.

Mason was happy to see Mitch with his friends and answered, "No." Some of these guys Mason had met from the neighborhood. "Hi, Mr. Morgan," one of the teens who'd played touch football with him, called out. They thought Mitch and his brothers were lucky to have Mason for a guardian. "Are you going to help coach football?' the boy asked bluntly.

"What! Who gave you that idea?" Mason was surprised.

"They always recruit the parents for as much as they can, so I just thought they'd recruit you since you'd been a star player in college," the boy explained.

Mitch overheard his friend and was worried. He came over then to apologize to Mason. "I didn't say a thing. Honest." He was afraid Mason would be mad, or at least upset about his friend's comment, but he wasn't.

Mason shrugged. This was all new to him. "It's okay. Let's just get your fees paid and meet Aiden and Mandi for lunch. I'm sure they are finished and waiting on us."

"I'm all paid up. I wrote my own check," Mitch explained. "Was that okay?"

"Sure... Lunches, too?"

"Yes, sir," Mitch said; he was proud that he remembered to pay for his lunches, also.

"Let's go, then," Mason said to all four teens.

Mitch turned and called out "See ya" to his friends and then left with his family.

"Hey, Mitch's homeroom teacher didn't meet you," Trenton remarked.

"Another time, Trenton; it will be okay," Mason told him as they exited the building.

LATER THAT AFTERNOON

Mason and Mandi were in agreement.

"Come inside, all of you. We want to have a discussion with you," Mason called them in from the field. Mandi had stuck a casserole in the oven, set the timer, and went to join them in the family room where they all looked pretty nervous.

Did something go wrong at the school during the registration? They were all worried.

"Is something wrong?" Kyler asked, studying Mason's face.

"Did we do something wrong?" Mitch asked at almost the same time, just as Mandi was entering the room. He was thinking of his friends comment about coaching and worried.

Mandi had heard both questions and felt their distress. She knew Mason's waiting on her was causing them to guess the wrong reason for this meeting. Shaking her head, she joined her husband.

"Nobody did anything wrong," Mason assured them. "We shouldn't have waited this long to do this. School officially starts tomorrow. Mandi and I have something to ask all of you. We want you to think seriously about this," Mason began.

"You're leaving, aren't you? I knew it was too good," Mitch cut in. "I knew you would." Mitch looked hurt, betrayed.

"Mitch, you're jumping to conclusions-the wrong ones, too. Please listen," Mandi told him. "Please," she repeated. He nodded, still downcast.

Mason spoke up, "This isn't easy for us. Then again it is. We've been here a month and in that time we have found something really important: you guys. All of you. We didn't think about it happening. Didn't plan on it. We just wanted to help…then," he paused as Mandi's hand came up to his lips. He reached for it and kissed her fingertips. In the past month these teens had seen them hug, kiss, joke, and tease each other as well as work together. They were in tune with each other and the guys were learning that they truly blended in everything they did.

Mandi took over. "This is a family meeting, dear, not an employee talk. You're taking too long." She smiled and he said "Hmm." "My turn," she said looking from Mason to the anxious faces of the five teens. "We have lost our hearts to all of you. We stayed to help and fell in love with each of you. Yes…we love each of you and it's time we said it out loud to all of you, not just ourselves. What we want to ask you is this: if we can stay here with you. Not just for a little while, but for a very long time is our request."

Mason spoke up again. "If you will have us, we want to be more than just your guardians. We want to adopt you, all of you and make it permanent."

Five pairs of eyes stared at them. Their faces registered shock. This was the last thing they expected. Each of them had geared their thinking to the Morgans leaving sometime, not wanting to stay very much longer. Now they had to decide what they wanted. They knew they didn't want the Morgans to leave. Each one had found security in having these two adults around. But, adoption had never entered their minds. Kids were adopted, not older teens, or so they thought. They instinctively knew that they had to agree and stick together.

Mason spoke again. If they put off the boys making a decision, gave them time to think about it, would that be on their side? "We don't expect you to say "Yes," or" No," right now. It's a big decision and we want you to be sure of the answer you give. We both decided that you needed to know how we feel."He changed his tactics. "I do have to leave for a couple weeks; business calls me away. But, remember, whenever Mandi or I or both of us are called away on business, we will return. As long as you want us or need us, we are yours. We love you and will not desert you.

"So think about our request. Talk it over together and when I return from my trip, you can tell us what you decide." Mason had spiked out his heart to them. Now it was up to them. He had not put any less into this decision than he had when he asked Mandi to marry him.

Mandi said. "Let's eat. I heard the timer on the oven go off…." As they headed toward the kitchen, Mandi continued, "Guys, if adoption scares you, it scares us, too. This is a new concept for all of us. This is a big step for us, but we feel right about it. If you don't, we won't desert you or hold it against any of you. We will still be around, if you want us to." Everyone was still, quiet, thinking as they followed her to the kitchen.

They were told to wait until Mason returned from his trip for their answer. They talked it over and over among themselves. Being adopted meant they'd always be together. It meant the Morgans wouldn't leave them. It meant they'd have parents again. They also admitted to each other that they not only liked the Morgans, they did love them. They did not want these adults to leave. These two new adults had won them over.

They were scared to commit. Had they seen the real Mason and Mandi living with them? Or, would their personalities change after they adopted them? Would being adopted mean they had to move to where the Morgans had been living? Where? When? So, they found it easy to put off voicing their decision for the two weeks that Mason was gone. They had school to adjust to again anyway.

They watched Mandi to see if, without Mason around, she'd be any different now after telling them about adoption. She wasn't. Mandi stepped up to all that was part of being a mother, taking care of them, working, without a complaint, with smiles and love.

TUESDAY

Mandi had the jitters. They were the ones going to school-all five of them. She was going to work as was usual. They seemed excited about being around their friends. Mitch would drive them all to school in the older minivan, dropping Aiden off at the junior high before going on to the high school. She would pick up Aiden after school daily as he got out a half hour before the highschoolers.

Mandi had made an appointment for Trenton's physical, but was nervous thinking of meeting this family doctor who knew the boys well. She felt like an outsider, more unsure of herself than before. She could face one hundred new employees in a new company easier.

THURSDAY

Today was the day-Trenton's physical-not hers, his, so there wasn't any reason for her to be nervous .But, she was. She'd let the school know about the appointment, that she'd pick him up a half hour early. She picked up Aiden after Trenton, met the doctor, found a way to relax about this aspect of parenthood. She made it through her first meeting with their doctor.

If she and Mason were to adopt these guys, they would be parents in the full sense. Wow! She was happy…nervous…excited…scared…ready. She loved them as much as she loved Mason in a different way. Mandi thought of this as she drove Trenton and Aiden home. At home, Mitch waited for her in the kitchen.

"Something bothering you?" she asked him as she pulled out meat for supper.

"Yeah, I'm sorry," he stopped.

"Sorry about what?" Mandi turned to Mitch. "It's okay, Mitch, just tell me. Don't give me a heart attack."

He grinned at that. She cared. "Well. I found out that my physical from last year won't work. I need a new one to play football. I'm sorry."

"Stop saying you're sorry and don't worry. I'll call and make the appointment; probably all of you will need new ones. Who knows-it's no big deal. I'm pretty sure I can handle this." She gave him a reassuring hug, and then sent him off to do his homework. She finished the supper preparation.

Chapter 4

FRIDAY

Mandi repeated what she made her normal send-off, "Drive carefully," she would tell Mitch. "You have five of my favorite guys in that car."

Everyday Mitch was energized by her words. "Yes, ma'am," he always answered, smiling. She'd wink at him, watch him drive away with his brothers.

This fourth day of school, Mason spelled out his feelings to his brothers. "We have to let them adopt us; we have to keep them around I...can't do all this on my own, guys. I didn't know how much was...is involved. She doesn't even complain, just adds something else to her list ...and takes care of it. I don't believe I could do that. I'd probably be yelling at you. Sorry... She's going to check and make doctor's appointments for all of us for school sports. I never thought about any of that. "No one answered him He didn't expect them to.

Mitch apologized to his brothers, "Sorry, guys, I'm venting and she's the one doing all the work." Mitch really found that he could appreciate the way that Mandi was taking care of them. She hadn't the experience that their mother had, yet she didn't shy away from it. To come in, take over, not complain, and do a great job impressed Mitch. His brothers, too, understood and were also in agreement.

"See you later, Aiden. Have a good day," Mitch said as he stopped at the junior high. Mitch dropped Aiden off, as usual, drove to the high school and parked.

It was easy to easy to get back into routine. At home, they knew the old rules should still stand. Each one found fresh baked cookies and milk and headed to their rooms to do their homework. They hated that the first week of school was full of homework and reports already.

Mandi baked cookies nightly after the boys were all in bed. She baked cupcakes and brownies, too, cut into squares. All were for after school or evening snacks.

It was Friday and Mandi was glad the week was over. She was preparing supper when the cell phone rang. Answering it was routine as she worked, tucking it close to her ear.

"How's it going?" was his first question.

Laughing at his unusual greeting, she responded, "Hello, I miss you too." Then she proceeded to fill him in, only this time the news was personal, not work related. "Trenton had his school physical yesterday. I forgot to take the guardianship papers with me. Didn't think about the doctor wanting to see them. And, I guess I'll need to make appointments for all the boys so they can play sports. Mitch told me his last year's physical was a month shy, so he needs one to play football. I guess all the boys will play a sport of some kind." She was rattling on, talking while preparing the evening meal, telling him everything at lightning speed as her hands worked with the food. But, he'd known her too long, caught on to the tiredness she wasn't even admitting to herself.

"You sound worn out and stressed, love. Are you okay? And, yes, I miss you very much. I'm so used to you being by my side." It was his turn to rattle on, but they really needed to talk about this decision to adopt as it was probably the most important one of their lives. "I've been thinking, hon: adopting these guys is really going to change our lives forever. Is it putting too much on you? Do you really want to, still? Tell me." Mason also knew that if they adopted these guys, they would be taking more trips separately; or, he would, more than she, be the one going. He didn't like that idea, but would have to accept it.

Mason waited for her answer. He was willing to do what she wanted, needed, even though he knew he didn't want to back out. Mandi smiled at the thought that they knew each other so well, that through the phone line, the tone of her voice alerted him to her lack of energy. She answered him, "Yes, I'm tired, but it's not a bad feeling. Yes, I still want to adopt these guys. I love them, Mason, with my whole heart, as much as I can love them."

Mason was relieved, but he knew her as well as she knew him, and had expected that answer. "Good, because I almost miss them as much as I miss you. How does that sound?" He admitted these feelings were new to him.

They confused him, but uplifted him at the same time. He could hear her laugh softly and the familiar sound was uplifting to his heart as well as his mood. "We are really in this forever, aren't we, love?"

She laughed, "That sounds wonderful. Aren't we the lucky ones? And, I'm not the least bit jealous, my love. I'll share you with all five of these guys as long as you feel the same as I do. We're a pair, aren't we?"

"As always, a pair, a team," he answered. She listened then as he told her of the troubles where he was. She continued to prepare the meal as she listened. She waited until he was through talking and asked for her opinion before she gave it. She hung up missing him even more, the tears filling her eyes and running down her cheeks. But, the supper meal didn't suffer, she still readied it.

Unbeknownst to her, Mitch had stood silently in the doorway. He heard most of what she said, guessed at Mason's side. She still loved them and wanted to adopt them. From one comment, he gathered that Mason was also willing to take all of them on. He couldn't feel any better hearing that. Whatever the man, her husband had said, Mitch had held his breath, watched her face smile at his words. Mr. Morgan wanted them; Mrs. Morgan wanted them. They wanted both Mr. and Mrs. Morgan. How lucky could the get?

Her back was to him as he entered the kitchen a few minutes later after waiting so she would not know he'd heard anything. He was shocked, "You're crying. Is everything okay?" Mitch was confused. The conversation he had heard was good, wasn't it? Then why was she crying? Since Mitch had only seen his mom cry a couple times and she had been upset or sad at those times, Mitch was unaccustomed to this display.

She nodded, smiled at him, and wiped her cheeks, "Everything is fine, really. I'm just feeling down because I talked to Mason. I miss him, but, I'll be fine. If he hadn't called, I'd have been fine. The Jock!" She smiled again at Mitch, then surprised him by pulling him into a hug. She hugged him close for only a minute, then released him and changed the subject. "What do you need, love?"

Mitch smiled. That was what she'd called her husband on the phone. He'd heard her. Love!-he liked it. "Nothing." He found his voice, just barely. "Just wanted a refill on my milk..."

She watched him fill his glass. "Save room for supper," she teased.

"No problem," he grinned. He surprised her by kissing her still wet cheek before he left.

She had to sit down: her knees went weak. She sat there smiling, one hand touching her cheek, smiling to herself, at herself, at nothing-oh, no, not nothing. This was definitely a milestone. Her heart was swelling inside. She knew it had to be. She sat there in a daze until the timer on the oven went off. It broke the spell.

She set the table, then called up the stairs, "Supper's ready, who's hungry?" Ten feet answered her call almost immediately. "Wash up, let's eat."

"Yes, ma'am," echoed down the stairs.

Saturday and Sunday were lazy days for the boys. They ate breakfast Saturday after sleeping in until after ten, and then disappeared outside to find their friends.

Mandi cooked the breakfast, cleaned the kitchen, and then vacuumed the front room, hallway, and living and family rooms areas. She needed to keep busy to keep from missing Mason so much. She dusted the downstairs rooms, did her own laundry, and then made lunch of sandwiches and fruit for them all. She had found out that if she sliced up the fruit, the boys ate it, but not if it was just sitting there on the table in a bowl. Personally, she didn't understand it, but it worked. As she was finishing up with the drinks, the teens trouped in.

"Oh, wow, thanks, I'm starved," Trenton said.

"Me, too," Brendon added.

"You're always hungry, so how could I ever tell the difference?" Mandi teased.

"Not me," Kyler said innocently as he sat in his usual spot.

"Ha, eat," she ordered this teen that was already taller than she.

"Thanks for everything," Mitch told her as he sat down.

"You are all welcome," Mandi stated as she joined them. As she ate, she watched each one.

Sunday, she took them to church, then shopping again for groceries for the next week. Forcing them to help her choose the menu items was not really 'forcing' as they were willing to let her know their likes and dislikes. Still tired from the last week, Mandi took them out to a nice restaurant so she didn't have to cook and everyone ate well.

MONDAY

Before they left for school, Mandi informed Mitch, "Mitch, I will be at the high school just before time to pick up Aiden. Make sure you give the car keys to Kyler and come out a half hour early. You did turn in that slip to get out for your physical last Friday? Right?"

Mitch nodded while finishing his breakfast, "Yes, ma'am, I did. I'll be ready."

"I need a slip signed," Brendon spoke up. "I almost forgot it." He went to retrieve it from his backpack. "It's for a field trip," he explained.

"Where to, hon?" she asked even as he was handing her the paper. Reading, she teased, "Oh, I don't know." She tried to keep her face straight.

"Huh? You have to sign it. I'll get in trouble," Brendon pleaded. He gave her a puppy dog look. She grinned and held out her hand for a pen which he gladly handed to her.

"A field trip, huh?" she said as she signed. "To the police station. Hmm."

"This is the first step to my getting my permit to drive. Does that scare you?" Brendon teased.

"Terrifies me, Brendon, but, boy, you forget the power I have here." She was looking at him sideways. "Do you really want to learn to drive?" She wiggled her eyebrows a little. "Well, let me think about this."

Brendon groaned, the others laughed.

Watching the clock, Mitch was beginning to fidget. He interrupted, "We gotta go, guys, or we'll be late and get detentions. Then she'll have something else to rib us about." He was grinning at her as he spoke.

Still holding Brendon's slip even though she'd already signed it, Mandi spoke, frowning, thinking, wanting to tease Brendon a little.

"Okay, guys, go. I'm just going to have to talk to Mason about this. Insurance premiums are going to go up." She laughed as she followed them out to the garage and the minivan they rode to school in.

That was another expense that Mitch hadn't given a thought to: car insurance for all of them driving. The Morgans were paying that also. They were buying the food everyone ate, hadn't used that new account they'd opened. Food and car insurance were a huge expense.

Before handing Brendon the paper, she said, "I need payment for signing this," she told him. When he gave her a confused look as he was reaching for the paper, she tapped her cheek with her finger. Embarrassed, Brendon kissed her cheek, took the paper and ducked into the car.

Mason called after they were all gone, telling her he'd be home Wednesday evening. At first they talked about all she'd done with the boys. Mason wanted to know all about them at home, and then he talked about the two stops he made, before asking about where she was in handling the newest factory. "How is the new factory running?" he asked.

"Fine. Everything seems to be running okay. No, I haven't decided who I think should be in charge when we can't. I have a feeling this will be our base from now on, for five years anyway." She laughed at his answer to that.

Mitch thought that if they had to move after the adoption was final; the boys would be coming with them just as in any normal family. His brother moved around and his family went with him. Mandi was with the boys and knew that moving was not an option. So when Mason said, "Love, we will be in charge. If we need to move, the boys will move with us, Right?" Mandi answered him, "Oh, you are new at this, my love. I've been here. I'm beginning to believe they are in control of our future, not the other way around. It's in a good way though," she laughed. I signed for Brendon to go on a field trip to get his driver's permit this morning. I made him pay me for signing that paper," she told him, not explaining the payment.

On the other side of the line Mason was frowning. "Okay, I'll bite: you made him pay? How?"

"I made him kiss my cheek. It embarrassed him, so I think I'll use that more often." She laughed, remembering, and then continued, "Hurry home. We all need you. I've been going in to work after the kids leave for school, working from eight until two-thirty, when I leave to pick up Aiden at school. I've taken two of the boys for physicals and I've got three more to do." She ended with, "The house is a mess. We need a housekeeper here-I'm catching myself coming and going, really."

His laughter stopped her rattling. "I love you. You sound like a mom. I love hearing your voice, even complaining. I will be home on Wednesday, I promise." He only wanted to reassure her he'd be home soon and be there to help. Home? When had he started to think of that place as home? As their home, even? He gave her his love as he hung up. Both went to work, different places, different states, even.

The work at the factory-office work-was work she felt very competent at. She was there by eight, ran the meeting at ten, made phone calls on what was supposed to be her lunch hour to other businesses they owned, but had to leave the spread sheets unfinished to pick up Mitch before Aiden for Mitch's doctor appointment for his sport's physical. This time she remembered and had the guardianship papers with her.

Back at the house by four-forty-five, she started supper, put in a load of the boys' laundry, and folded another load. They definitely needed a housekeeper; she needed help.

Homework done by the boys, supper over and cleaned up, laundry folded, Mandi headed for the bedroom for a shower to ease her sore tired muscles. The boys were engrossed in a TV program. Dressed in thin tan cotton slacks and a sleeveless pink top, she lay down on the bed a minute to stretch out. And, she fell sound asleep. A knock on her door woke her up. "Are you okay?" Mitch was standing in the open doorway. "We missed you."

"I just took a shower." She began, but Mitch's smile stopped her.

Mitch grinned, "And, fell asleep, huh? You must have been tired, 'cause we are on our way to bed now. It's ten p.m., goodnight." Still grinning, he left the doorway.

Ten, she thought? Was he right? Yes, the clock beside the bed agreed with him. She'd been asleep over two hours. And, could easily go back to that restful place. So…she put on her night clothes after checking to make sure the boys had locked everything up.

Mason had better agree on a housekeeper, none of the house had been cleaned since Saturday, except for the kitchen and some of the laundry, of course. Worse, she didn't get to enjoy her sons tonight. Did she just call them her 'sons' in her mind? She did. The thought had her grinning as she climbed the stairs to her bed. She liked that thought. They were her sons in her heart already. Being tired was okay as long as she had these young men to love.

WEDNESDAY

Mandi had prepared Mason's favorite meal, lasagna-two extra big pans of it ready to cook when she and Aiden arrived home. While Aiden sat in the kitchen, as usual, doing his homework, she unloaded the dishwasher, made a batch of brownies-a large triple batch-and they smelled so tempting. Aiden sighed, enjoying the aroma as he tried to concentrate on his homework. Mandi was ready, she set the table and made tea and lemonade.

The other four came in as usual, had to settle for the cookies for their snacks instead of the brownies, and went to their rooms to do their homework. All as usual, not as usual, they talked about today being a very important day: Mr. Morgan was coming home. Would he be here by suppertime? They hurried their homework in case he was early.

Mandi was as excited as when they were dating. After she'd found out that the football star quarterback turned her insides every way but loose when he kissed her! After she'd finally admitted to herself that he was sure handsome in and out of his uniform! After four years of dating throughout her college, she was his and his alone, and he was hers.

It was a good thing she knew what she was doing with the meal, concentrating would have been hard otherwise.

While Aiden sat at the table, doing his homework, and talking about his day, about some visitors had come to the school and he was still excited. He kept stopping his work to tell her more about his day. She loved every minute of his chatter.

Mandi couldn't wait. She couldn't be still. Mason was coming home –here-to her. This was their home now, her with these young men. For how long, they hadn't decided. At least until Mitch graduated, but then, Kyler would be a senior; after that it would be Brendon, then Trenton, finally Aiden, which would mean five years. They were committing themselves to five years. Yeah, they could handle that. It was the everyday stuff they would need help with because they had never been parents before. So, she couldn't wait for many reasons.

If the boys wanted them to stay, they would because that was what they wanted, too. She could find NO reason to doubt that was not what they wanted; their actions seemed to say they wanted and needed Mason and Mandi around. They'd been asking daily when he was coming home. That had to mean they missed him, and wanted him back.

She remembered when the boys had come through tonight, listening to their endless chatter:

Brandon was caught in the middle of, "And, he said we could."

"Yeah, you would," Kyler had interrupted him.

"I can if I want," Brendon had added.

"So can I" Trenton had offered up.

"You are too young," Mitch said.

"Am not!"

"Are, too!"

"Yeah, you are," came from another.

"Welcome home, guys," she interrupted their tirade. Aiden had laughed as his brothers stopped and realized they weren't alone.

Then: "Brownies! You made us brownies. Wow! Thanks." Kyler saw them first and just headed straight toward them.

"Don't touch," Mandi had said, "They are the desert for after supper."

"Oh, come on!" Come on was dragged out.

"Ahh, really?"

"How could you tempt us like that?"

All four had had comments, along with puppy dog hungry looks on their faces, but she held out. "You'll live," she laughed. "Milk and cookies will suffice. Homework, guys, supper's in the oven." They acted like she'd hurt them, mistreated them somehow, but filled their hands with glasses of milk and the cookies as usual, and then left her alone with Aiden. She'd listened to their footsteps on the stairs, could hear their voices, but not make out the words. So, she just smiled, was happy.

By five, she heard a car pull up, and knew it should be Mason's. The RV had taken up residence beside the garage, leaving the driveway open. It no longer blocked the street. Mason had driven the sportier car, leaving the minivans for use at home, so he was there shutting off the engine as Mandi came to the doorway. He sat for a minute, looking at the house his mind was calling home. His wife, his family was inside. Yes, he was home and very glad to be there, too.

When Mandi had heard the car, she hurried to the door and met him on the porch with the tightest hug she could. They kissed like newlyweds, coming up for air, then kissing again. Both were deliriously happy to be together again.

Without thinking of what he was saying, Aiden followed her out of the kitchen. He went to the stairs and called out to his brothers, "Dad's home." He then ran to the front door, wanting his turn with the man whom he wanted to really be his dad. But Mandi was Mason's only thought for almost five minutes. He'd missed her badly. They had always traveled together until this time. By the time Mason could make himself free himself from his wife, and she could force her arms to relax their hold on her husband, all five teens were on the porch.

Mason looked at the teens and smiled. "I missed you guys so much, I didn't know it was possible, He hugged each one of them, Aiden first as he was ready and jumped into Mason's arms. No one was embarrassed to be hugged. "Let's go inside, I think the neighbors have seen enough," Mason stated.

"I don't care what the neighbors think," Mitch told him and found he really meant it. He smiled at Mason. It spoke volumes to him, telling him he'd changed. They all had.

"Everything okay where you went now? You were gone longer than you said," Kyler announced.

Mason narrowed his eyes at Kyler, studying him. Really! He thought. You're asking me? He only said, "I know. Everything is okay there now. Very good. How about here? Anything I should know about"

"One thing, I guess," Mitch began. Mason searched the lads face for that one thing. What did he mean? Could it have anything to do with their proposal?

Mitch grinned, looking from one brother to the other. All nodded very slightly. Mason's eyes didn't leave Mitch's face. "Aiden said it," Mitch told him, nodding. Mason looked at Aiden as Mitch continued, "He said, 'Dad's home', and he was right. You are here-home."

Mason's heart swelled. He looked at Mandi, from her to the other boys, then back to Mitch. "Thank you," he whispered. His brain couldn't come up with anything else. "Thank you all," he repeated. They were all five on him again, close enough to touch. He looked at Mandi, over the boys' heads. "Did you know?" he asked. He meant about the boys decisions to agree to the adoptions and she knew that was what he meant, and she just shook her head, tears clouding her vision. Somehow, they made it into the house, no one particularly sure how. They were all inside crowding around Mason, welcoming him, and Mitch realized that Mandi had been the one around for the past two weeks, taking care of them daily.

He turned to her. "Are you tired of us yet? You are the one who was here for us these past two weeks, thank you for that. Do you still want us?" He was smiling at her.

"You know I want you, brat," she said as she hugged him.

Pretending shock, Mitch called out. "Brat! Did you just call me a brat?" He looked at his brothers, then at Mason. "Dad, Mom just called me a brat!!" He said it like this was really something, and in a way it was; this interaction was fun, something knew to them all. They had seen Mason and Mandi interact, but had not been included as yet. Mitch knew that calling Mason and Mandi dad and mom felt so real, even though it had been such a short time since his parents' deaths. He'd longed for this to be, and not just so they would handle the financial side of things. From the first day he had met them, he felt a connection. He remembered how he hadn't wanted them to leave, was glad they had agreed to stay and help. He couldn't explain that feeling as it had never happened before, nor could he forget it. Being there, it gave him comfort. Mitch simply accepted that, and knew his brothers did, too.

Mason laughed, took a few steps toward the lad, "Boy, if she ever calls you a 'jock', you're in deep trouble. Deep, lad, I want you to understand that," Mason said the words, warning him, but smiling.

"Don't worry, dear, you will always be my only jock." Mandi quipped, as the timer on the oven interrupted their teasing.

Mason turned toward the kitchen, "Babe, I am hungry, skipped lunch I was so busy, and then wanted to leave because I was in a hurry to get home." He'd just called this place home out loud. "Is that lasagna I smell? Oh, baby, I love your lasagna," Mason said. "There had better be lots!"

Mandi laughed. "I sure missed you, too. And, there's plenty, I'm sure." She kissed him again. "Let's eat while it is hot."

"And brownies, too, Dad," Kyler said. "Mom wouldn't let us touch the brownies after school; she made us wait for you."

"Brownies, too, guys this is serious, let's go wash up."

THURSDAY

They had made love after the boys were all asleep until they too had to sleep, woke up early in each other's arms and came together again. "I missed you so much," they told each other over and over as they were not used to being separated, not at all. Finally sedated and happy for now, Mason rose and took his shower while she lay there contented and relaxed. Her eyes were closed; she stretched and opened them to find him there smiling down at her, a towel around his hips, his hair still wet and mussed from the shower. She licked her lips and smiled back, pushed aside the sheet and stood up, wrapping her arms around him, snuggling close.

"Good morning, my love," she whispered, kissing away the water dripping from his hair onto his neck.

He kissed her hungrily; she wiggled closer and the towel dropped. "The boys won't get a home cooked breakfast this morning, I'm betting," he smiled as he spoke. Mason was ready to perform again, there was no doubt about that when the towel dropped, but he had to go and mention the boys and breakfast and put a damper on that.

At least for her, the mood was broken. "Oh…they will if I hurry and shower. Get dressed, mister," she laughed, releasing him, leaving him hot and cold at the same time. He shivered, sighed, then began dressing. A knock on the door interrupted his finishing. He answered it, sliding his shirt onto his arms. "Good morning, Trenton is something wrong?" he asked the lad who looked sheepish.

"No, sir, not really. Should we just eat cereal this morning? We don't really care, sir, honest. It is okay," He was nervous because his teenage mind had imagined what they were doing and even though he knew it was okay because they were married, he was not used to his imagination taking this route with adults-it was reserved for movies and people he didn't live with. His parents had never done more than a quick kiss as his dad left for work in front of them. They also had acted like they were too old for any hanky-panky stuff. Somehow, Trenton was sure these two were not too old for that.

Mason smiled, guessed at the boy's discomfort because of previous reactions. Their parents must have done NOTHING in front of them or in private for all of them to be so uptight every time he touched or kissed Mandi. How in the world they ever had these five sons Mason did not know. How did these guys think their parents conceived them, he wanted to know? Oh, they were just going to have to get used to it, he decided. "Relax, Trenton, Mandi is in the shower. And, I don't care if you eat cereal this morning, if that's what you guys want. That's fine, Mandi'll live." He teased. "I'll be right down."

"Yes, sir," Trenton said, and, then added, "Dad."

Mason shook his head at the lad, as he finished buttoning his shirt, then slipped his socked feet into a pair of loafers. Following the boys down, he knew Mandi wasn't far behind as he'd heard the shower shut off as he closed the door. Standing in the kitchen doorway, he watched their progress. One boy was putting bread into the toaster while another pulled out a couple boxes of cereal Mason didn't even know they had. The lad sat them on the table as his brother got the milk out. A fourth brother had the bowls and spoons for all of them. The first guy went to the frig for the butter for the toast and had a knife poised to slather the bread with the butter after it was toasted. They were all doing fine. Mason smiled as he watched. He spoke, "Do you think that because I'm back, it means Mandi won't be cooking breakfast anymore?" He couldn't help teasing them.

"Uh, no, sir, we just thought she needed a break," Brendon told him.

"Hmm," Mason thought his mind awhirl.

"Yeah, she wears herself thin doing for us and working. And, she hasn't asked much of us," Kyler added, pouring glasses of milk for everyone. He glanced at Mason to see how he was taking that declaration, but Mason only bit his lip, and frowned.

Chapter 5

Mason's thoughts were on Kyler's statement. What were they doing other than going to school and their homework? As a kid he'd had chores that had to be done daily or else he was in trouble. Hadn't it been that way here...before? They weren't lazy, he was sure- just accepting of all she was doing. Normal teenage reactions, to let someone else do the work, it was, and he knew that. He hadn't forgotten his teenage years. Thoughts poured into his brain as they did while at work. What had the boys done those first few weeks both he and Mandi had been here? Mason was trying to remember, but found those thoughts only on getting to know the boys and helping them,

"She's always up first and has breakfast all ready when we come down, then she goes to work after we go to school. We wanted to give her a break. That's okay, isn't it?" Mitch asked as he put a stack of buttered toast on the table and sat down.

Mason nodded, "Of course it is alright, and thoughtful. Thank you, guys. I could see how tired she was last night. Today, I am going to find someone to come in to help with the housework. We have a weekly maid in California when we're there and the same at our home in New York. I'm here now to help with the rest, so her load will be lighter. I didn't mean to leave her with all the responsibility. It just happened." Mason started the coffee as he talked. It was time for him to be a parent; Mandi had been doing it for the past few weeks while he was gone. He knew that and was willing to do just that. He and Mandi had talked about it, but then he had to leave, and she'd been hit with all the running and the work. To make this work, they all had to work together, He knew that they knew that, but being young they'd let her take over and do it all, he'd bet. He added another thought to their already loaded brains, "You guys do need to know that there will be times when we both, Mandi and I, will have to travel together. We will both be gone for a short time, a week or two, and you five will have to work together and help each other and us. Understand?" He leaned against the counter as he spoke, waiting for the coffee to brew, watching them eat, knowing they had heard everything he had just said.

"We can help, Dad. We will. We are not helpless. And, we'll be fine when you have to be gone. Honest!" Mitch promised.

They were pouring second helpings of cereal when Mandi waked in.

"I've been replaced already," Mandi laughed. "Sorry, guys. Hmm, I smell coffee, thank you, babe."

"We're practicing for when you both have to be gone sometimes…to show you we can do it okay." Aiden explained, making Mandi frown with confusion.

She looked at Mason, knowing he must have said something to them of that nature, and then back at the full table. "Don't need me anymore, huh?" she teased, seeing them eating cereal and toast hungrily.

"He didn't mean that," Kyler said, worried about her feelings.

She patted Kyler's back as she accepted a cup of coffee from Mason.

"You could put more bread in for toast. " Brendon teased.

"Oh, thank you, dear, my pleasure," she laughed again, reaching around Mason for the bread. She pressed herself close, very close. He reacted, put his coffee cup down and wrapped his arms around her. She had some difficulty putting the bread into the four slice toaster, but finally managed as he kissed her ear and her neck. When she pushed the lever down on the toaster, he claimed her lips. "You're hindering progress, mister," she said when he released her. He only laughed and kissed her again.

Aiden piped up, "Mom, don't ever listen to these guys. They're full of…whatever. He admitted, "I wanted to call you mom and they told me I couldn't. I had to wait until dad came home. I was not happy with their way."

Mandi kissed the top of Aiden's head, "I love you." She told him. "I love all of you very much, even Mr. Morgan over there. She was grinning as she went to sit between Kyler and Aiden in an empty chair. Mason was also enjoying the teasing. When the toast popped up, it was Mason who buttered it and put it on the empty toast plate. He then put in four more slices. He was hungry, too, and the hot toast smelled good. He leaned against the counter, tipped the cup to his lips, and sipped the hot liquid, all the while watching the table full of teens downing cereal, toast, and milk. Watching his wife, his love, sitting there with them, happy, made him happy, deliriously so. He was tuned in to his thoughts and not to the conversation until…he came back to the present when Brendon asked, "Why didn't you like dad at first? You know- when you first met in college? Remember what you told us?"

Where'd that come from? Mason thought. What had he just missed? But, Mandi remembered. "Well," she began, "I thought he was a conceded jock, a show off, that he thought he was too good for others not as good at sports as he was. All those cheerleaders crowding around him like an idol rubbed me the wrong way, I guess. I just didn't see the real Mason at first."

"She was jealous," Mason teased, winking at her. She just shook her head and rolled her eyes.

"The cheerleaders were all after him, Huh?" Mitch mused, glancing at his new dad. He had a growing case of idol worship himself. Both Mason and Mandi could see that. Mason laughed at Mitch's words, at all the memories, and at youth.

"Is he still a show-off?" Trenton asked, ducking because he thought Mason was going to pop him on the head or something similar. All Mason did was put more toast on the table, leaving one in his hand to eat. Smiling, he looked at Mandi, "Only for my love," he teased, making her smile, too. "You guys had better get going." Mandi motioned toward the kitchen clock above the sink." Okay," they agreed, hurrying off, leaving everything on the table. Eyeing the mess, Mason frowned. Yes, they might be running late today because of all the conversation. But Mason knew that they could clean up after themselves, not leave this mess for Mandi to take care of. Had they left this mess every morning? Had she made them help while he was gone? He didn't know, intended to ask. So he did.

"Usually they do help put their own dishes up for me," Mandi told him.

"What time have you been going in to the factory office, my love?" Mason asked his questions when it was just the two of them.

"Usually now or in a half hour, depending on what clean up I do," she told him, watching his eyes. They told her of his thoughts. And, he was right, she knew.

"Hey, they can and will learn to clean up after themselves some. There isn't any reason for them not to. I know they were full of questions today, and because of that were running late, but things will calm down when they feel secure with us here." Mason said this unnecessarily, knowing he and Mandi thought alike most of the time.

Together Mason and Mandi put everything away and into the sink, and straightened up the room. Then the two of them left for work. At the factory,

Mandi caught Mason up on this plant, showed him how well it was working. They also talked about other businesses they owned, and those he had visited just lately. Their computers were running full out all day-until two-thirty.

"It's time to pick up Aiden," she announced, shutting down her computer."

"Why do we have to pick up Aiden, love?" Mason wondered, also shutting down his laptop.

"He gets out at two-forty-five, a half hour before the others at the high school. I don't want him standing around waiting for that time. And, I like picking him up."

"Then let's go, love," Mason smiled as he picked up his laptop and hers.

Aiden was happy to see the two of them together. He ran to the car with a grin on his face. "Hi," he said, hopping in the back.

"Hi, yourself. Did you have a good day?"

"Yes, Mom, but I've got a big history test tomorrow. I gotta study."

Dinnertime brought more questions, more inquiring into Mason's and Mandi's pasts in order to know them better.

"Are your parents still alive?" Trenton asked Mandi. He was thinking of more grandparents. None of them had thought about siblings or parents as far as Mason or Mandi were concerned-until now.

Mandi had always been open with Mason about her childhood when they had gotten to know each other. It made no difference to Mason and it shouldn't to these guys. They knew that not all families were on the best of terms, so she explained hers. "My mother and I are not close. We rarely see each other, the opposite of Mason's. She still lives where I was born and raised, near Chicago. My parents divorced when I was ten. Dad remarried and I haven't seen him since I was fifteen. He said I'd never be anyone important, never be any better than my mother whom he learned to hate, I believe because of what she did and was. Well, of course, I had to prove him wrong." She shrugged. "Maybe that was his intent: to make me work harder to be different than she was. It worked-I worked hard, very hard to get where I am today. I am who I am because of his words and I am happy. I couldn't be happier."

"Sorry, I guess that was not a good topic," Mitch apologized.

"It's okay, really, Mitch, half my life ago and like I said I'm stronger than that kid who wanted his love. I never look back at that life except to know it made me who I am. Education is the key to a good life, guys. Don't forget that."

"Yes ma'am, we know that," Trenton told her. "We just want to get to know all about you. You said you weren't close to your mom. Can you tell us why? Was she like your dad? Did she desert you, you?"

"You're a really great mom no matter what. You are!" Kyler added.

"Thank you, Kyler. Well…my mom started out as this business man's mistress, but when she became pregnant with me, she forced him to marry her, coerced him, bribed him, whatever you want to call it. He married her, but never gave up his other mistresses even though mom hung in there trying for ten years. They fought constantly, loudly. They weren't happy together. She liked the security of his money and made sure she got her share in the end. Neither ever loved each other, or me. She used me to hang onto him, and then in the end all she wanted was his money."

Mandi continued, "When I was young, I went to private schools, the best education available. He had to pay for it all. He paid child support and alimony through the nose to be rid of us. I went to Southern Cal because it was a great school and it was expensive, made him pay for it all, for all my education because he said I'd never make it. That way he would know he was wrong. I never wanted to see him and knew he didn't want to see me. I just wanted to prove I could make it and I did. End of story." Mandi was not affected by her tale as the boys thought. To her it was just a story from the past, a past that was long gone. Both Mason and Mandi knew that these boys had the right to know them if they were expected to trust them, so neither were bothered by the interrogation.

Mason knew Mandi's story and how she'd overcome everything to become a great person in his mind. He told the boys, "We are where we are today because we both decided to be the best we could be. That's all that matters. And real love," Mason said.

"How about your family, Dad? Are you close? Are they going to be shocked to find out about us? Tell us about them," Kyler prodded.

"Shocked would be one way to describe their reactions, I suppose." Mason smirked. He told them, "I have an older brother, Marty, and a younger sister, Miranda or Randie. Marty is married to Carol and they have a boy and a girl, Chuck and Tonya. They're fifteen and thirteen, I believe."

"You believe? You don't know for sure?" Trenton teased, grinning.

"Mandi," Mason pleaded, "Save me."

She just laughed, "They are fifteen and thirteen. Chuck is probably six-foot-two now and very skinny. The taller that kid gets, the skinnier he gets.

He has light brown hair like Mason and Marty. They look a lot alike but I think Mason's cuter." Mandi wasn't prejudice, not much.

Mason shook his head, looked at the teens around them. At their eyes, at their faces. They were absorbing all of this.

"You don't know their ages very well. Does that mean you don't see them often?" Brendon asked. Mason shook his head at this remark as it was true for a different reason. "Not too often since they live in France," he told them.

"France. The country?" Aiden was wide-eyed.

Mason smiled at the wide eyes and shocked expression on Aiden's face. "Yes, Aiden, France, the country. He, my brother, is working over there. He does more traveling for his company than I do. But, he's been in France for about two years, I think." Mason took a breath. They were all finished eating, but no one wanted to leave the table, so he continued telling about his family. "Now, my younger sister lives in the U.S. with her husband and three kids, one boy and two girls. David is nine, Julie is six, and Gina's two. She lives in Billings, Nevada, not far from our parents. That's where I was born and raised, went to school until I went away to college, and met Mandi."

As long as the boys could think of something to ask, both adults were truthful and straight-forward in answering them. Forget the TV tonight, the boys thought, talking to their new parents was more exciting. Even though they hadn't set a date yet or met with a judge to make it legal, to the boys it was. To Mason and Mandi, it was something special, something neither of them had ever thought would happen. To Mason and Mandi it still seemed illusive, even scary.

SATURDAY

"What shall we do today?" Mandi asked Mason as they were finishing breakfast. Mason had surprised the boys by making waffles lathered with whipped cream and berries.

"This is really good. I've never had waffles like this before," Kyler said as he finished his plateful. His brothers nodded.

"Filling and delicious, I loved them. Thanks, Dad," Brendon added.

"Me, too! Will you fix them again, another day, Please, Dad?" Aiden pleaded, downing his milk.

"Sure, no problem, I can do that," Mason told them. He was eyeing these guys dressed in shorts, ready to head out to play, he thought. But, he had another job in mind. "As you're finishing, I want to talk," Mason announced. They all looked up at him, wondering. He continued, "When you are finished eating from now on, I want you to start cleaning off your own plates from the table. Just pile them in the sink, that's all I ask." He watched them shrug, nod, and accept his suggestion. "There's no reason you can't do that, guys," he finished.

Mandi had told him that they usually did do that unless they were in a hurry or had their minds on something they thought important enough to override that duty. She hadn't complained so they didn't realize they were slacking. She let Mason take charge of this situation.

Mason turned his attention to the oldest of the teens, "Mitch, what did you normally do on a Saturday morning after breakfast?" Mason's gaze was on Mitch's eyes which the lad immediately dropped to his lap. Uh oh, he thought. He was the oldest; he had to tell the truth. He found his voice.

"Mornings… clean our rooms, gather our dirty laundry and any dishes that we had left in our rooms," he responded. He looked at the man sitting at the end of the table in a parental seat, like the dad they wanted him to be. He sounded just like their dad would have if he were still here, and they all knew he was right to say what he was saying this morning. No one wanted to admit it, but Mason was right.

"And you hated it, I suppose," Mason surmised, leaning back a little in his chair.

"Of course," Kyler answered, "but we did it, because we had to."

Mason glanced at Kyler, took in his honest words, but now he would ask a harder question. "Have any of you done any of this in the past month?" Mason let his eyes travel over all five of them and knew the answer. Everyone's eyes averted away from Mason as he met theirs and settled in their laps. Yes, he knew the answer. Now, here I go, he thought. "Whose job is it to keep your rooms clean?" he asked, though no one was looking at him. All of a sudden their laps were all important. He waited patiently.

"It was Mitch who answered, fessing up as he knew he should, "Ours," he said. He didn't want to admit it but felt compelled to do so; he felt the responsibility rested on him. This was what Mason and Mandi had seen in him all along-responsibility.

Mason switched to a different approach to the problem. "I was gone for two weeks. Who do you think did my laundry? Did you see me bring in a bag full of dirty laundry for Mandi to wash? Do you think, but most importantly did I think she should wait on me?" He saw a few heads shake, a little; they were listening. They understood, from Mitch down to Aiden. He watched as that bomb fell into their laps. He wasn't asking of them anything he himself didn't do himself, and without complaining either.

A couple of the boys shrugged, not knowing what to say. Well, they knew what they should say, Mason could tell; they were too embarrassed now to open up. A couple more shook their heads, in the same position. No one had a real answer for him, so he told them, "I did my own laundry, guys. It didn't hurt me one bit. It sure didn't make me any less of a man. Understand?" He kept his voice even and low, not condemning.

Nods were reluctant, but they came finally. Now they felt awkward, he knew. But, he wasn't finished. "Now, I'll ask again. Have your rooms been cleaned in the past month?"

"No, sir, not really," Kyler admitted. His brothers looked at him.

"No, sir, but they aren't really dirty either," Trenton added quickly.

Mason studied Kyler and Trenton, then the other three. Mitch looked ashamed, as the oldest, he wanted to be the role model. Mitch was feeling very guilty. That wasn't what Mason wanted from any of them. He had to finish what he started, but he wanted, no, needed to do it without piling guilt on them.

"Now, what shall we do about this…situation?"

"I guess we're cleaning our rooms this morning," Trenton spoke, downcast.

"Do you like clean clothes?" Mason asked.

"Of course," Brendon said. He sighed.

"Well…" Mason left it open.

Reluctantly, Starting with Mitch, the oldest, the leader, Mr. Responsibility, they each took their dishes to the sink and then left the room. No one said anything verbally, but their body language told their stories. They weren't happy; they would much rather go outside while the weather was still nice.

"Please strip your beds and bring me that laundry first," Mandi told them as they were leaving the room. She thought she heard a "Yes, ma'am," or two, but wasn't sure.

Their fun times had just ended and reality had set in, each of them was old enough to know that Mason was right. They'd let Mandi do it all while Mason was gone and that had been wrong. Their biological parents would not have let that happen. They knew the rules than and the consequences for breaking any of those rules. They each understood that following the rules honored their biological parents as well as these two new adults they wanted to keep around as parents. With these thoughts in their heads, they went about the cleaning as they should have been doing all along.

Mandi started toward the sink to do the dishes. For the past two weeks Mandi had kept the downstairs clean, done the laundry and the cooking, worked at least thirty hours at the plant, and kept the bathrooms clean and sanitary. She hadn't complained; nor had she asked anything of them. She knew that was wrong; she should have made them do some chores. She believed in that totally. But she had wanted to get to know them personally and spend as much time with them as possible. They had her heart. Having been afraid that on her husband's return, they might be leaving and losing the teens forever, she had relished her time with them. She was building memories.

Mason stood up, helped her load the dishwasher. As he did so, he said, "I know I'm the bad guy, hon, because I've brought them down out of the cloud, but it has to be,"

Mandi's thoughts were on the boys' reactions and if they were now sorry she and Mason had come into their lives. The memories she had stored in her heart would be there forever. She also knew Mason was right. They had both been raised to help. She needed to tell him so.

"I know I was wrong in not asking anything of them, but I thought you and I would be leaving her now and I wanted as many memories as I could store up and take with me. I'm sorry, love, really." Mandi apologized, closing the dishwasher and starting it.

Before Mason could answer her, Mitch spoke up, "You weren't wrong, Mom," he said, "Not really, we were. We all know we were just being lazy, not doing our part. But we loved having you here. We were also afraid that you would change your minds and not want to stay and, boy did we blow it. We should have been on our best behavior to convince you we were worth having you. We all love you very much, you are a wonderful mom and too good to be treated that way. We owe you an apology for our misbehavior. We were the ones in the wrong, not you, letting you do so much.

"Aiden's the only one her young enough to be excused," Mitch declared. In his arms were his sheets and comforter, ready for the laundry. He had heard them talking as he neared the kitchen. "And, you're not the bad guy, Dad. It's time for us to accept our responsibility as part of this family. We do want to be a family." He smiled as he entered the kitchen, and headed for the laundry room. "I'll put these in the washer. I even know how to start it, we all do. Then I'll clean my room every week from now on and keep it that way, like I was taught to do." Mitch said, walking into the laundry area with his sheets.

Mason smiled, "I don't expect perfection, Mitch. If you were perfect, you wouldn't need us. Not at all."

At that Mitch smiled, "I guess you're right. And we do need you…both." When his things were washing, he headed back upstairs to clean his room.

One by one the others came down with their sheets and comforters, carrying them into the laundry room, dropping them on the floor. The washer was still going. Trenton was the last one down and by then the washer was finished. Because he had been taught and without being told knew he should, he put Mitch's wet load into the dryer and started his own.

Mason and Mandi had left the kitchen area, each to do their own chores. Mason had gone outside and decided to mow the lawn. It had been over two weeks, he knew, so it was quite a job to tackle.

Mandi was in the family room cleaning and dusting. She ordered pizzas to be delivered at noon to please their guys and to thank them for being cooperative.

Now their rooms were clean for the first time since their parents' deaths. Everyone was proud that they had accomplished the task they didn't really like, without balking. They had admitted to each other that this was the right thing to do. Their mother had taught them to be responsible. She would be very unhappy with them for being lazy, but proud of them for doing what was right.

Today they were starting over. They needed to show this second set of parents that they were very lucky to have a chance with them; they needed to show them how much they cared by cooperating-most of the time, at least, to the best of their teenage abilities. They wanted this to work.

Mandi carried Mitch's dry laundry to his room after putting someone's form the washer to the dryer and someone else's into the washer. Mitch's room was spotless, the windows open, a cross breeze blowing the brown curtains slightly. It was truly a beautiful day, inside and out. Standing on one side of the bed, she helped him make it up.

"I can do it," he had said.

"I know and I can help. It's faster and I want to tell you I'm proud of you. Your room smells clean. That's healthier, you know." She smiled at him as they tucked the sheets in.

He was smiling, too, "Thanks for being here for us. For staying. For caring enough." It was time for him to confess something that had been eating at him for almost the whole two weeks. "You know…I'm the one who told the others not to call you 'mom' until dad came home and we knew you'd both stay. I was afraid you'd leave and we'd lose two moms and two dads before we even had you. I'm sorry. I feel so bad not trusting you."

"Don't feel bad…brat. I love you." She smiled.

He grinned broadly. "Did you just call me a 'brat' again?" he teased. Then he added, "As long as I'm your 'brat' it's perfect." He walked around the freshly made bed and hugged her.

She hugged him close, and then told him he could keep an eye on the washer and dryer, so she could do something else. "I put someone's sheets in the dryer and someone else's in the washer," she told him.

"I can handle that, Mom," Mitch promised and went to do so.

Mason cut the acre of grass that was their yard, then the field where they played ball, and trimmed around the trees in the yard. Then he cleaned and put the mower away before the pizzas arrived. He had started on the garage, just opened up the big overhead doors when the pizzas arrived.

With Mandi's and Mitch's help, all the beds were made up with clean smelling linens and comforters. Each teen had picked up, dusted and swept their floors. All the carpets were a short pile, each room in a different color. All the rooms had two windows for cross ventilation, a dresser, a desk, and a double bed. Not much else in a way of furnishings except for their collections of normal teen items: a few books, notebooks, pens, pencils, footballs, pictures. None of them had computers in their rooms, but they all had a stereo system as Mandi saw a few CD's on Mitch's desk.

"Hey, guys, there's pizzas down here," Mitch called upstairs to his brothers as he'd helped Mason carry them in. Mandi came down with the boys as she was working on her and Mason's room.

Chapter 6

THURSDAY

"Are you nervous? Mason asked Mandi, "Because I sure am. I've never done anything like this before. And, it's definitely permanent… forever, right?" He didn't wait for her to answer him, just continued, "We're in deep, aren't we?...but I can't wait either. It is the right thing to do and I want it more than anything." Mason took a deep breath and let Mandi take over with his tie. His fingers were all thumbs today. He dropped his hands to his side and made himself stand still. Then he kissed her lips lightly. "Thank you," he said.

As she tied his tie, she told him, "Yes, I'm nervous, but I'm also floating on a cloud. To really make it official, make it real is a blessing," Mandi finished his tie as she talked. She hadn't seen her husband nervous too many times .She handed Mason her necklace to fasten and gave him her back side, holding up her hair. She took a couple deep breaths while he was snapping the clasp.

"We will be on time, right?" Mason asked.

"Yes, dear, we will be fine. We will pick up Aiden, and then meet the others at the high school. They will follow us to the court house. We will have plenty of time. Our appointment is at four o'clock. All the paperwork is or will be ready," Mandi assured him.

Mason voiced his biggest fear: "The boys won't change their minds when we get there and decide not to let us adopt them, will they?" Mandi shook her shoulder length auburn hair and smiled at him. Her green eyes met his green eyes that matched his deep green shirt and two-toned green tie. Four emeralds full of love for each other, and five teens gave each other comfort.

They drove to the junior high and parked in their usual place, waited for Aiden to come out.

"Today's the day-finally-isn't it?" Aiden asked as he climbed into one of the middle seats and tossed his backpack on the third seat behind him. He was excited. "We sign the papers and we really are one family. Right? Do I get to change my last name? Do I?" He was almost bouncing in his seat with excitement.

Mandi turned half way to face Aiden. "Do you want to change your last name, Aiden? It's up to you," she told him.

He didn't hesitate, "Yes, I do," he answered, excitement showing; "If you and dad are legally my mom and dad, I want your last name and mine to be the same. Then everyone will believe you are really my mom and dad. I'm not sure my friends understand that I want to do this, that it is the right thing to do."

Mason watched him in the rear view mirror as he drove out of the busy parking lot, heading to the high school. He smiled at the boy's words. They made him proud, his heart swelled. He hadn't felt this overjoyed since Mandi said 'yes' she'd marry him. He was no longer nervous because he was sure all these guys felt the same way. Now he was confident the usual 'Mason-style' confidence!

"Aiden, do you remember I told you that you could have both last names legally to remember your birth parents?" Mason spoke quietly, reminding the boy of their previous conversations.

Aiden nodded, "Yes, Dad, I do, but do I have to say both names every time or can I just be Aiden Morgan?"

"I like that." He smiled at Mason in the mirror. He had done some thinking about that and was unsure. Most of his friends had only one last name. He'd have two. That was different. Aiden didn't like being different. He didn't like the label of being an orphan. Without parents. He didn't like having to say his mom and dad were dead. That hurt. He wanted a live mom and dad to love him. He knew Mason and Mandi loved him. Their actions as well as their words told him that. He wanted to be their son and have them be his real mom and dad.

"We will ask the judge that question, if you wish, but my guess is 'no' you have a middle name that you don't use all the time. To me it would be the same. Okay?" Mandi was trying to reassure him, calm him down some.

"Yes, thank you. Let's hurry. I don't want to be late." Aiden was afraid that if they were late, they'd miss out and not get adopted. That would hurt.

"We won't be late, Aiden. We are meeting your brothers first, and then going to the courthouse," Mandi calmly reminded him.

He buckled up as they were finally out of the parking lot. There were many students leaving in many vehicles and progress was always slow. Aiden was in a hurry, but could do nothing too.

To make conversation as he drove, Mason told Mandi, "I had lunch with Randie while I was away." Randie was his younger sister, Miranda, whom he thought a lot of. He wasn't crazy about her husband, Ryan, but accepted him, until now. Usually they could get along okay at family functions. Ryan wasn't any fonder of Mason or his brother Marty, so the feelings were mutual. Mason's last visit with his sister proved to him that Ryan wasn't worthy of his sister; especially after this last visit, he knew.

Mason was close to both his brother and his sister. He and Marty had always been very protective of their sister. Mason had always idolized his older brother, even though as siblings they had had a few disagreements… every week growing up.

He didn't want to tell Mandi about his sister's problems right now, but wasn't surprised when Mandi caught his reluctance and said she thought his sister was having a rough time.

Mason shook his head, not feeling good about the news. "Listen, hon, we'll talk." He left it open. They didn't need bad news today.

Mandi knew without him saying any more that Randie was hurting. She had problems with her husband and their marriage.

Mason pulled into the high school lot and found where Mitch had parked the car he drove himself and his brothers to school in- their biological mother's minivan. Mason had talked about replacing it with a newer vehicle, but Mandi vetoed him. This one still ran good. She had said, "That school bout parking lot is a mess with so many kids driving. I see no reason for a new vehicle that we'd all worry about getting damaged. As long as this one is running fine and is safe for Mitch to drive, that is." She was right and Mason knew it, had conceded.

"Mason, we have a few minutes. Tell me about Randie," Mandi said as he turned off the ignition. She unbuckled and turned toward him cocking her head. She would listen.

He took a long minute to react.

"Ryan left her, didn't he?" Mandi deduced. She knew the couple had been unhappy back when she had gotten pregnant with their third one. But they had stayed together.

Mason nodded. "She said they were separating, contemplating a divorce. She's pretty broken up about it, but he deserves whatever happens. "Taking a breath, he continued, "The kids are a mess. They are testing her and she's so down she's letting them get by with anything and everything. She's upset, mad, hurt, and didn't like my comments on her handling the kids. I don't wish to see Randie anytime soon," he finished. Mason felt very protective of his sister and Mandi knew it. In front of Aiden, he did not admit that Randie had told him he was not a parent and did not understand, so he had told her about these boys they wanted to adopt. She had been shocked and very surprised at his admission.

Mandi listened attentively as she cared for his sister almost as much as he did. Aiden was listening, too, of course. He WAS in the car with them. How could he not hear? They were talking as if they'd forgotten they weren't alone, as if he wasn't there. But, he didn't care. He wanted to know about this sister of Mason's named Randie. That sure was a different name for a girl, he thought. Aiden decided to let them know he's heard. He wanted to know what had happened to his new dad's sister, his aunt now.

"Why did your sister's husband leave her?" Aiden wasn't sure they would even hear at first. But, they did. Mason turned to ward Aiden, "I'm sorry, son, it's a long story. My sister and her husband have had problems for three years or so. She's thinking of ending their marriage. He's moved out. It's not a good situation right now. We have better, more important things to think about today."

Aiden smiled. He'd called him 'son' and that made Aiden happy, and proud. He loved this new dad…and mom.

A knock behind Mason on the driver door window had them all turning. Mason hit the button to roll down the window after restarting the car. "Hi, guys, we're ready," Mason announced unnecessarily.

Grins met his words. "Yeah, we could tell. You were busy talking…about what? What did we miss?" Kyler teased.

"We were talking about how slow you guys are," Mason teased back. He pulled away as they all jumped in the other van, knowing that Mitch would follow him.

At the courthouse, formalities were followed. The judge interviewed each boy individually in his chambers, asking them questions: were they in agreement with the adoption? At their ages, they had some say. Did they know the legalities involved? Did they really like or love Mason and Mandi? And, did they believe that Mason and Mandi loved them? "Do you understand the finality of adoption, young man?" the judge asked each boy in turn. Satisfied that all the lads understood and really wanted him to approve their adoptions, and satisfied also that Mason and Mandi cared enough to adopt and care for five teenagers, not just one or two, the judge signed all the papers. The boys and their new parents also signed their names to the documents. A notary put a seal on them and gave Mason and Mandi a copy for themselves to keep. It was done. It was real. They were the parents of five teenagers.

Mason took his family out to a nice restaurant to celebrate. They were all happy and talking about the future. To most anyone who paid any attention to them, they were a family, not a new one as there were so many of them and the boys were older. Both Mason and Mandi were proud to call these boys theirs now as well as a little afraid of what was in store for them as parents.

On the way home Mason's cell phone rang; he took it out, checked the ID and frowned. "Who is it?" Mandi asked, noting his facial expression. She almost reached for the phone, but he breathed out one word-"Randie." He was debating answering it-the phone won as it kept insisting.

"Hi, Randie…wait…slow down…hey, girl, hang on." With a huge sigh, he pulled the car to the side of the road and put it in park. He was still listening as he stopped the car. "Say that again," he was frowning as he spoke, closing his eyes, listening to her wild insistent raving, trying to make it all straight in his head. Finally, he said, "I'll call you back in and hour or less…I know…I'll do what I can, sis. Bye." Closing the phone, he leaned his head back against the head rest; his eyes closed, his breathing heavy, his mind awhirl.

Mandi was not used to being in the dark as to Mason's thoughts or feelings, whether personal or business. She waited a full minute before speaking. Her voice brought him back to the present. "Mason, what's wrong?" He turned to her. Took in his surroundings, where he'd pulled over, remembered the boys behind him and came back to the present. He came back to his wife and sons. They were his priority now. He smiled at her, stiffly, but it was a smile.

"Nothing I can't handle later. Let's go home. This is our special day. I don't want it ruined," Mason said as he put the car in gear and pulled back onto the road. Mitch had also pulled off the road, parked behind the couple who were his new parents, legally now, and waited, worried. All the guys were wondering what was going on, if something was wrong with one of them up in that car or if there was car trouble. Mitch sat there not sure whether to wait it out for Mason to come to him, or to get out and check on them. He really was worrying, unsure of the proper approach, when Mason put his blinker on and turned back onto the road home. Mitch followed.

"What's wrong?" were the first words out of Mitch's mouth once they were all out of the cars, parked in the garage. "Dad. Mom. What's wrong? It has to be something. You were stopped for at least five long minutes." Mitch was frantic.

Mason turned to their oldest son legally now, intending on relieving his fears. "Calm down. I didn't mean to alarm you. I had a phone call and pulled over to give the caller my full attention. Sorry to have worried you."

Mitch relaxed, so did the others who had been with him. Aiden was quiet. He knew more than his dad was telling. His new aunt had a problem- and, she wanted their dad to help her solve it. He knew that. He looked at his dad to see if he should just keep quiet. Inside the house, it was Mandi who confronted Mason.

"Tell me all she said, Mason," she demanded quietly. He eyed her closely, trying to decide if he wanted to talk in front of their new sons. They'd find out some day, he thought. He hated to involve them, today of all days. He wanted today to remain special. Her call had tainted it for him-and that hurt. It also hurt to think of shutting his sister out, to not help her when he could, when she was hurting. He was a better man, a better brother than that. Mandi reached out and took his hand and started walking. He followed her to the table. She sat. He sat. All five teens followed them to the table where they also sat down, prepared to hear the story.

Mason looked at Mandi. He looked at each of their sons, sighed, took a deep breath. "I'm sorry, guys," Mason began; "I'm really sorry that this happened today, but I have no control over every situation."

"We understand, Dad, really, but we're family and a family sticks together. We're with you," Kyler told him. "You can tell us the bad news as well as any good news. We will stand by you. You stood by us."

"How'd I get so lucky, love?" His words were directed at his wife, but his eyes were on Kyler. Perceptive, the lad was. They all were, he was sure. They knew instinctively it wasn't good news because of the way he and Mandi were acting. How could they be so in tune already?

It took all of Kyler's willpower to keep his eyes on his new dad. He'd learned to love and respect this man in a very short time. But, he knew Mason had a big worry on his mind…now…and it had nothing to do with them. It had to do with that phone call he had received on the way home.

Mason sighed, said, "You will know soon, anyway, but I didn't want to ruin our day. Remember today because it will always be special. Hey, I love you guys very much."

"You're hedging, Dad, I'm good at that." Brendon was grinning.

Mason grinned back at Brendon. He said, "I'll remember that." Continuing, Mason said, "The truth is: I don't want to be a part of this, but I will have to, anyway, because it involves my sister, and," Mason looked from one to the other, then he continued, "Kyler's right, a family sticks together through good and bad. So, I have to do what I can to help her, now that she needs me to."

Kyler smiled at Mason. Before any of them could ask him to tell the story, Mason did. "While we were waiting on you four to get out of school today, I told Mandi that I'd had lunch with my sister while I was away. I was close to her home and called her. She and her husband have not had an easy time these past few years. Now they are separated, getting a divorce."

"That's too bad. We're sorry," Brendon said for them all. "Divorce is hard. I have friends whose parents are divorced. It's no fun."

"Me, too," Trenton added. "It causes turmoil for everyone."

Mason smiled again. Oh how his love was growing for these guys. He knew he loved Mandi more than life itself, but somehow his love for these guys was very close to what he felt for her. He wasn't sure how that could be or how it happened so fast, but he truly believed it had.

"Yes, it does," he agreed. "It almost never is peacefully handled. In my sister's case, she and her husband are not on friendly terms," Mason told them as gently as he could. The truth was much worse.

"You mean that they're fighting, don't you, Dad?" Mitch asked.

Mason shook his head, he hated to admit to the truth, but now that he had started this with them, he was not going to lie to them, not for any reason would he lie. Mason and Mandi had always told each other the truth, no matter what they had to face, they did it together. "It's even worse than that, son, much worse. They have three kids who are caught in the middle, being torn apart by both parents. Both want full custody," he told them. "They each want to turn the kids against one or the other. If any of your friends have ever really talked, then you know the emotional merry-go=round that creates," he told them. They nodded, all quiet.

Mandi had listened carefully. "What did Ryan do?" Mandi asked. She wanted to know the details of the phone call and expected Mason to tell her, as usual. The boys all seemed willing to accept what Mason had said. Mandi concluded that they were in no way keeping any secrets from these young men.

Mason looked at his wife. "He's filed an injunction to try and prove she's an unfit mother, so he can get sole custody."

"That's bull, Mason, she's a good mother," Mandi interrupted. She was mad.

"I know sweetheart, but right now she's a wreck. She needs someone to help her and I'm not sure I'm the right person for the job." Mason answered.

"What can you do other than be there and offer her moral support?" Mandi asked. "And, maybe that's all she needs right now-her big brother," she added with a smile.

He scoffed, then shrugged before he said, "Except for helping her choose the best lawyer to help her, nothing, I guess. She's scared, very worried, and she has the right to be. I will help her find a better lawyer than she has right now. But, she has to get it together. She has to take control of her life and her kids. Or else, she will lose them and her own sanity, probably. He has a good job. She doesn't work. That will hurt her if she doesn't play her cards right." He found no reason to sugarcoat the situation.

Mandi understood. She and Mason both had college educations. Miranda had been eighteen when she graduated from high school and married Ryan who was three years older. Ryan had been the sole supporter of their little family, the man of the house. "Are you going?" she asked quietly.

Mason put his elbows on the table and covered his face with his hands. He took a few deep breaths before he looked at Mandi. He saw only her-now-his mate, his love. He knew his answer. She knew his answer, but she asked anyway.

"Yes...no...I don't know...Yes. I have to." He looked at Mandi, but he was seeing his little sister, whom he'd always been there for-to protect and love.

"Randie is used to me just taking off whenever she calls...so, she calls. I can't just do that anymore. I don't," he stopped because he couldn't say he didn't want to. She was his little sister, always would be. He would always want to help her, but he and Mandi had just committed themselves to these guys and he wanted more than even he understood to be there for them, steady, to be a dad.

Mandi also understood his unspoken words; his feelings were hers, too. Her hands came up on top of her husband's and he looked at her. "I love you," he whispered. She smiled. "I love you." That was all she had to say.

"Does your sister know about us, Dad?" Mitch asked. He and his brothers wanted to be a real part of this.

The mood was broken. Mason turned to Mitch. "Of course she does, yes. I told her all about each of you when I met her for lunch last week. That's when she told me her news. I wasn't shocked really. I knew they weren't happy, not anymore, not for a long time." Mason was still saddened by the fact that his sister must suffer and the children, too, who were innocents.

"So, we have a new aunt and cousins, huh?" Kyler said, his eyebrows lifting, teasing, but not teasing.

"Her kids are nine, six, and two, sorry nowhere near your ages," Mason told them.

"That's okay." Brendon shrugged.

"Hey, we could all pile in the RV and go with you. I want to go riding in that thing," Aiden announced. "Couldn't we?" His face brightened.

"You have school tomorrow," Mason reminded him with a smile. "I'd love to take you, but it's not a pleasant time."

"Ah, we could miss one day," Aiden said. His face fell at the rejection of his idea.

"Good try, Aiden," Trenton said, "maybe next time it'll work. Maybe next time he'll want us to go." He was smiling, teasing and his brothers recognized it, but he was sure Mandi didn't know by her shocked expression.

Mandi hadn't ever scolded any of them, but here she was…"Trenton," Mandi scolded, "You will not say or think that again."

Trenton looked contrite. "I'm sorry. I was teasing him, honest."

"Then," Mandi told him, "You chose the wrong wording, son." There was not a sign of her scolding tone this time. Her tone was softer.

"It is okay, Trenton," Mason assured. "I took no offence, but I also agree with Mandi about your wording." Mason saw both sides; he tried to be the peacemaker. "Guys, this is our special evening. What would you like to do? I'll listen to all requests."

Mitch spoke up, his mind still on the phone call that had upset his new dad. Mitch was sure he had Mason pegged. "Dad, don't you need to go… to help your sister Randie? She called you, right?" Mitch didn't want to be part of his dad not helping his new aunt.

"Mitch, son, there is no way I could get a flight out of here tonight, so I'll not worry any more tonight. I'll make reservations in the morning, just for the weekend, I hope. Like I said, this is our evening to celebrate. Okay?"

Mitch nodded. Good…he didn't want Mason to go, not tonight.

Brendon, too, was worried, but he was also glad to hear that their new dad would rather be with them, at least for tonight. "Do you like to play card games?" he asked.

Of course Trenton was also listening and ready. He wanted to feel that things were going to be close to normal again. "Yeah," he echoed. "We haven't done that in a long time. I know where the cards are." He jumped up.

"We all do, dope," Kyler said.

"Hey, he's not a dope; I don't like that," Mandi scolded another one, but it really went unnoticed by everyone but Mason who smiled at her.

Kyler heard her, rolled his eyes and said, "Sorry," but she wondered if he meant it. They were just getting to know the boys' ways, their little differences in personalities.

Mandi popped popcorn and they played card games together, relaxing, laughing, and teasing. Mason and Mandi truly enjoyed this part of parenthood, and were pretty sure the boys did as well. At nine-thirty, Aiden was excused to take his shower and go to bed for school tomorrow. Although he didn't really want to quit playing, he did so without much fuss. The evening and all its currents had worn him out.

The others followed soon after, one by one, as was their normal routine with school. The fated phone call was not mentioned again by anyone, but it was also not forgotten by any of them. The boys all knew that their new dad would be leaving tomorrow to help his sister and hoped he was right about only being gone for the weekend. They just got him back and now he had to leave again. Life wasn't fair. Sometimes. They all knew that. That didn't make any of them feel better as they prepared for school the next morning.

Chapter 7

FRIDAY

Mason was lucky and found a flight out early after the boys were all off to school. Mandi drove Mason to the airport, and then made her appearance at both schools with her copy of the adoption papers. This changed their status from guardians to parents and changed the last names of all five teens from Cooke to Morgan.

She worked as normal, picked up Aiden as usual, fixed supper as usual, and had a relaxing evening with her sons watching a movie before they all finally were tired and headed up to bed. Then, she talked to Mason after they were all asleep.

Mason had been a father for only one day, now he had to be a brother again. He had had years of experience in being a brother, very little in being a dad-he knew that, and thought about it during the flight. He was an uncle to Marty's two and Randie's three, but that was different. He had memories of his dad with him and Marty and memories of his brother with his son. Mason could draw from these two men some, but these new sons of his and Mandi's were teenagers. Therein lay the difference. Also, there were five of them, brothers; Mason expected them to stick together, to stand together up for each other. Yeah-like he and Marty had, as teens, he remembered. They would also have disagreements among themselves; he also knew that, although they hadn't seemed to do so in front of him or Mandi-yet. At least, they hadn't seen any squabbles-they would surface, he was sure of that. So, on the phone, Mason and Mandi talked and talked about all of these things until they were both exhausted.

SATURDAY

Mason called early. The boys were all cleaning their rooms as they were back on their regular routines, the way they'd been raised. Without fuss or complaint, they had headed up after enjoying a big hot breakfast. This made Mandi's life a little easier as they were more helpful in other ways also.

Mason wanted to know if it were possible to switch places. Could she come and help his sister recover her control over her life and her children.

"I really think you are more qualified than I am as a woman, love." She agreed with his assessment; women listened to women. Randie would accept her opinion, maybe more than Mason's, now that Mason had told her she must learn to handle life as a single parent. Mandi told her husband she would do her best to help Randie. Mason had also hired a top notch lawyer who specialized in this.

"If my coming will help Randie, I will be glad to do it. You know that." Mandi wanted to do whatever was best for her sister-in-law without hurting the sons they had just adopted. She had always felt a closeness to Randie from the beginning.

"I'll be home before supper time. My flight should arrive around four. We'll talk to the guys together. I want their insight. I don't want to hurt what we are building up."

She let to pick up Aiden around three-fifteen. He was at a school friend's house. She had a casserole ready and in the oven, the timer set. Supper was ready when Mason and Mandi and Aiden walked in. The table was set, and the guys, their sons, were waiting, ready to eat.

Mason looked at Mandi, grinned, and said, "You know, I could get used to this, start to expect it." No one understood the importance of his statement, until they sat down to eat and were told of the switch. Mandi was needed to help out with Randie and her kids, to help get her life back in the right perspective.

"When's Mom leaving?" Mitch asked. He was trying to understand. He was mature enough to know she wasn't deserting them; she was just being a good friend to her husband's sister.

"I made a plane reservation for four tomorrow," Mandi relayed. "I'll call you as often as I can. I'll miss you, all of you. You know I haven't been away from any of you since I met you except for work and school. Don't get along too well without me. Okay?" She grinned at them.

Sure that getting along without her was impossible and that they all felt the same one of them told her so. "Impossible," Kyler told her. We need you."

"Are you going to cook, Dad?" Mitch teased, "Or, do we eat out for two weeks?"

Mason scoffed at Mitch's words. "You, young man, will find out that you'll owe me an apology. I am a very good cook. Ask Mandi. We used to always take turns, or do it together." Mason pretended to be offended, but his eyes were twinkling with amusement. "And, where did you get the two weeks anyway? It shouldn't be that long," He remarked.

"Yeah, cereal for breakfast," Kyler teased, "Pizza for dinner." He was enjoying the teasing atmosphere. Both he and his brothers knew they would never have teased their biological father in this manner. No way!

"Another doubter, I shall remember that, boy." Mason warned. "Have you forgotten my waffles already?" He shook his head.

She left on Sunday as planned. The boys ate cheeseburgers cooked on the grill that evening. Easy solution.

MONDAY

Mason knew that each teen had his own alarm and got up to that on his own. So, he rose, showered, dressed, and headed to the kitchen, and his coffee. He started breakfast and turned on his laptop. Mandi had left on time yesterday and he and the boys were on good terms. He had cooked cheese hamburgers on the outside grill that evening then played catch with the football until dusk. He had successfully tired the guys out and they all headed in to showers and beds. Alone, he called his sister's home to talk to Mandi and get a update on what she thought about the situation. She walked outside to be alone and tell Mason her real thoughts. She also reassured him she felt comfortable that everything would be fine.

Mason checked programs he had running on several holdings, drank his coffee, made a long distance phone call to one of the businesses and was just hanging up when the teens trooped in.

Aiden greeted him with, "Dad, I need lunch money."

"Good morning to you. That I believe I can handle. All I need is the checkbook." Mason glanced up from his laptop.

Mitch followed Aiden in with, "It's in the desk drawer in Dad's office. I mean yours and mom's desk now." He looked sheepish over the slip-up, but technically he wasn't wrong. There was truth in the statement. It was his dad's desk and his dad's office as Mason was Mitch's dad now, wasn't he? Mason just smiled at Mitch as he added, "I'll get it for you."

Mason let Mitch's slip disappear and only replied, "Thank you, Mitch. Everyone else sit and eat." Mason hadn't stood up when they entered, but he had lowered his laptop and gave them his attention. He enjoyed the camaraderie he was seeing.

Mason had never before understood why parents enjoyed just watching their offspring until he met these five young men who fascinated him. He couldn't get enough. Not yet. Maybe not ever. And, that was good.

So Mason smiled and talked to all of them until they had to leave. He wrote a check out for Aiden for his school lunches, made sure the others were okay, and felt very lonely when they left.

"You won't forget to pick me up after school, will you?" Aiden asked on his way to the garage and the car.

"No, of course not; have a good day," Mason assured him smiling. How could I ever forget any of you, he asked himself?

Work didn't ease that feeling of loneliness. On Monday or Tuesday, but by Wednesday he was more relaxed, busy with the routine. Meals were easy; he had told them that he was a good cook. Proving that was easy. Loving them was easy. They were cooperative, got along most of the time with each other, did what he asked, and were responsible.

Missing Mandi tore at him, even though she called every day. Now he knew what she'd gone through those two weeks he'd been gone. All six of her men took their turns talking to her. Mason was first and last. Then he called her back after the boys were all asleep and they really talked. She could openly tell him about his sister and the kids.

Mason was right. Mandi had been a great help getting Randi to pull herself together and be the woman and the mother she was meant to be: a good mother who truly loved her children.

Mason had also hired the best lawyer his money could buy. Between the lawyer and Mandi, Randie was accepting of her plight.

Mandi said "Randie wants you to know you were right-she was just feeling sorry for herself as well as being furious with Ryan for his underhandedness."

"Thanks, love," Mason said. He felt better now because he'd been hard on his sister when he'd been there. "I'm glad you are able to help her."

As they talked they made plans for Randie and her children to all come and spend Christmas with them where they were now with these new sons. Randie and her children would finally meet her new nephews. Mandi raved about them all the time. They both agreed that the boys would be happy to meet Randie and her three. By Christmas, everything would be settled for Randie and the trip would be good for her children.

SATURDAY

"What time does Mom's plane arrive?" Mitch asked at a breakfast of bacon, eggs and toast. They hadn't eaten cereal once in the past six days.

"Not until two, so you have plenty of time to clean your rooms," Mason told them.

"Ah, thanks a lot for spoiling our day off," Kyler retorted. They had all been responsible about keeping their rooms clean after their talk with Mitch upon his return not long ago, but Kyler wanted to razz him anyway.

"Welcome to adulthood and responsibility, lad. I have no idea what a day off is." But his words were softened by his smile as served them t hot breakfast. Again.

Mitch cleaned the kitchen after they all left to strip their beds and clean their rooms. He cut the grass and did the trimming. He ran a few programs on his computer as the boys took turns with laundering their bedding. Soon their beds were all made and their rooms cleaned. Mason wanted the boys to know he would never ask them to do what he wouldn't, so when the washer was finally empty, he stripped his own bedding and loaded the washer again. Mason vacuumed the carpet in his bedroom and straightened up what he had messed during the week.

Today lunch was sandwiches, chips and fresh fruit. Easy to fix and serve while he did other chores. After lunch, he sent them outside. "Get some rays. Run off some energy," he told them.

"How about you, Dad?" Brendon asked.

"I'll be out later. Go on." He watched them run out the door.

Mason and Mandi always shared the chores at their former homes, so he was accustomed to doing them. He was fast. He was efficient. He vacuumed the downstairs before putting the sweeper away. Then Mason headed out to the garage and backed out the new minivan, then honked. "Who's going with me?" he called out. All five said "Goodbye" to their friends and came running to the van, pilling in.

At the airport, they all waited, excited. She was coming back to them. When they saw her, they all ran to meet her. Mason was as excited as the boys. He waited until last to hug her and kiss her, but not patiently. She winked at him a couple times as she took turns hugging each of their sons. It still seemed surreal to call these guys their sons, but she loved it.

Mandi kept her story about Randie and her three children g-rated in front of the sons they had adopted. She assured Mason that everything would be fine now as long as Randie stayed on track. Mandi was optimistic. As usual, they would talk when the others were all asleep.

SUNDAY

They had made it a part of every Sunday to take the boys to the church they were used to going to, after a good breakfast and before a light lunch. Then the boys would join others from the neighborhood in the field as usual.

Mason backed both minivans out of the garage. He could hear voices, laughter and marveled that he could pick out his sons' voices from the others. That surprised him. He ran a bucket full of soapy water and carried it between the two vehicles. Mitch and Kyler were in the driveway when he turned on the hose to wet down the cars.

"Need help or just company?" Mitch smiled.

"You want to get wet, huh?" Mason teased, tossing them a couple rags. Together all three vehicles were washed and waxed, the two minivans and the smaller car.

"The RV's next," Mitch announced when they were through.

"Very funny," Mitch said.

"You're on your own, Dad," Kyler added.

"We're outa here." Mitch said. They hightailed it out to the field.

"Ah, come on, what's wrong?" Mason teased as he picked up the rags and bucket. He had no intention of washing the RV by hand, just teasing his sons, something he found he enjoyed, watching their expressions. "I'll remember your desertion," he laughed. "Have fun."

Mason cleaned the already clean garage as Mandi was fixing dinner. She wasn't surprised that the house was clean when she came home as she and Mason had always shared any housework or laundry among themselves before they moved here. Sharing responsibility for home and work was beneficial and she knew it would still be. Their new sons would learn that taking care of a home and all it entailed was everyone's responsibility. Supper almost ready, she joined Mason in the garage as he was finishing.

"You can pull one van in while I pull the other one in, okay?" He greeted her with a kiss.

"You did a good job, sir; they shine," she praised, teasing, smiling.

He grinned. "I had help. Mitch and Kyler stopped their play to help. They are good guys." Mason walked out with her to the vans.

"I agree. We are very lucky." Mandi said as they both pulled the vans into their parking space, and then covered the smaller car with a protective topper.

The guys saw their parents outside and came over. They were getting hungry and so were their friends, so everyone was heading homeward.

"Okay, if you guys take showers, I'll promise to feed you," Mason teased. He had been teasing them all day, somehow, so they just shook their heads and went to take their showers. No problem.

The next five school and work days passed quickly and uneventfully. Mason wondered when they would face problems, when he would see disagreements among these five, or when one would balk at something he said or asked them to do. So far it hadn't happened.

SATURDAY

Mason joined the boys outside after lunch for a game of touch football. None of them had any mercy on him because of his age. So, by the time his cell phone rang a couple hours later, he was breathless when he answered it. He knew it was his brother Marty by the ID.

"Hello," he managed to get out.

"You okay?" Marty asked, worried.

"Yeah, fine," Mason took a deep breath. "Getting my tail whipped by a gang of highschoolers, but otherwise…" He laughed.

"So, it's really true. You did adopt some high school kids?" His brother questioned. "I leave the country and you fall prey," he teased. The camaraderie between the brothers was easy. Marty had grown up teasing his younger brother and found it comfortable as an adult.

As Mason listened he paced, getting away from the noisy teens to give his attention to his brother. He listened, he answered-he liked what he heard.

"Yeah, it's true. Mandi and I fell for these guys. Where are you?…You are? That's great…Riverton. Yes.…I didn't know I needed your permission…That is possible…We'd love it. You know that, bro…Give me a call when you are close." He laughed. "Yes, it is on the map…okay I will. Bye." Hanging up, he turned around, everyone was watching him. He'd have bet they had all been listening in to his side trying to find out who took his attention away from the game. Mason saw inquisitive expressions on all the faces toward him. To cover up, he asked the obvious: "Can't play without me for a couple minutes, huh?"

When he walked back toward the group of teens, the questions began. It took all Mason's reserve to keep a straight face.

"Who was that?" Kyler asked.

"Was that your sister?" Mitch asked at the same time.

"No, it was not my sister; it was my brother." Mason kept his answer short on purpose.

"Why?" Trenton asked.

"He wanted to call and talk to me."

"Why?" Mitch asked.

"To tell me he's back in the states." Mason left that one open, his own voice almost a question.

"Why?" Kyler again.

"His job brought him back. What is this? An interrogation? Let's play football. We're running out of daylight here, guys." The rest they could here later.

Realizing that was all the answers they were going to get for now, they shrugged it off and resumed the game. Until Mandi called out supper was ready, then all the kids dispersed to their homes for replenishment.

Inside Mitch and Kyler cornered Mason as they were all washing their hands.

"Okay, Dad, who was that really-on the phone out there?" Mitch asked.

"Yeah, we need to know," Kyler added.

Mason eyed the teen. "Need to know? There are quite a few things you will need to know, lad, but my phone calls are not among them." When Mason paused, he saw Kyler's eyes widen. He took a different approach as the boy apologized.

"Sorry, Dad, we were just worrying," Kyler said, feeling liked he'd overstepped, but they had always been able to ask anything. He was a little confused.

"There's also nothing for any of you to worry about. That's my job, and Mandi's. She and I will do our best to lesson your worries." He hung up the towel he'd dried his hands on, then continued, "Now, as to the phone call, I will explain that at the dinner table." He left the boys watching him.

"He's sure different from dad, isn't he?" Kyler looked at Mitch.

"Yeah, dad would have smacked each of us for even thinking we could question him on anything like that," Mitch told his brother. The others agreed. All hurried to the table.

"He's being sneaky, that's what I think," Mitch said as they were at the dining room door. He knew his brothers agreed, again.

They were all sitting at the table; Mason had said a prayer and food was being passed.

"I got a phone call while we were out there," Mason began. Mandi looked up at him.

"Really,' was all she said. She knew how to be patient with his moods.

All eyes went from Mason to Mandi, then back to Mason, waiting, not as patient as Mandi.

"Had a noisy audience, too" Mason informed her. Now she knew why he was dragging this out. Ornery, yes, he was. "Looks like we might have some company in the next week or so."

"Oh, do I need to know who this company is?" Mandi asked. As she said "need to know," Mitch and Kyler looked at each other. Mandi saw their look and knew Mason was doing this to tease them.

She shook her head. "Mason," she demanded in a little stronger tone.

Mason laughed. "It was Marty who called. He and his family are back in the states and want to drop by. I accepted."

Mandi gave her husband a look. He read it well. They knew each other's moods and thoughts.

"Marty's like you there, dear, he doesn't just drop by. He has an agenda."

Again Mason laughed. "Okay, so we are alike. You knew that ten years ago when you married me," he stated. Serious, he continued, "I don't know his agenda, except for Riverton. He'll call when they zero in on our location.

"I do believe everyone's hungry and the food is cooling off. I like my food hot," Mason said to close the subject.

"I'll call Carol… later…Eat." Mandi smiled.

Mason shook his head. He didn't argue with her. He ate, so did everyone else.

Halfway through the meal, Mason brought up another topic. "I do believe that new movie you were talking about yesterday is playing. Do you want to go see it?"

Mandi looked up. "Yes, I do. When?"

"You name it, love; I'll even buy you popcorn," he teased.

"Oh, you big spender, you. Maybe I'll go with someone else." She looked around the room.

"Oh, no," Mitch said, "leave us out of this, please."

Mason and Mandi both laughed. "I'm teasing," Mandi told Mitch.

"I hope so," Mitch said. He went back to his plate of food.

SUNDAY

The day passed as every other Sunday since the Morgans had come to town. The boys survived another week of school knowing that they had company coming that they had never met. Relatives. They had relatives from their birth parents, some they hadn't seen since the funeral. Relatives that had not called since the funeral. Now they would have relatives that would care about them, or at least that was what they wanted to believe.

Chapter 8

THE NEXT WEEK

SATURDAY

"Will they be here before we're done?" Aiden wanted to know. Both adults knew Aiden meant Marty and his family. The boys were nervous about meeting Mason's brother and his family. Excited, too, because this was part of their family now. They wanted to impress Mason and Mandi and that meant impressing Marty, too. They had learned that Mason and Marty were close and could easily understand that closeness as they held onto it themselves, after the death of their parents.

"Depends on who's driving, Marty or Carol," Mason teased.

He was almost always in a good mood, Mitch thought. Was his brother like that, too?

Mason turned his attention from his youngest son's question to his wife and the upcoming noon meal. Of course she was surprised by his question. "What are we having for lunch?" he asked.

Mandi gave him a quizzical look. "I haven't even got the breakfast dishes in the dishwasher yet. Gracious, what do you want me to fix, dear?" Mandi turned from the sink to face her husband. She was confused. What in the world was he talking about? She frowned at him, narrowing her eyes, waiting.

Of course all five teens were as interested as she was in this conversation. Whenever Mason and Mandi acted a little different, each lad watched to see how they were reacting to each other. They knew adults fought sometimes and waited for it happen with Mason and Mandi. So far it hadn't happened.

"You're not having a fight, are you?" Brendon asked, worried.

Mason and Mandi both shook their heads simultaneously. "No." They both answered together, then laughed. She still wanted an answer form Mason and he was being so evasive, but she was insistent

"What did you tell Marty?" Mandi asked the question, very suspicious.

Mason grinned. "He asked if your manicotti was still the best. I simply said it was." Masson answered.

So, now she had her answer; she would clobber him-if she had the time. "So, I'd better go to the store, so that I can make manicotti for lunch, right? Hmm, thanks for the warning."

"The pleasure is all mine, love," Mason blew her a kiss and left the room. Everyone followed him out.

The boys cleaned their rooms and helped Mason with the yard and the cars and the garage while Mandi did the shopping, and prepared the lunch in a clean kitchen. That meant Mason had to do the downstairs vacuuming and their bedroom. He didn't balk.

There were only six bedrooms in this house, all occupied. Where was this visiting family going to sleep? The boys didn't know. They thought that some of them would have to double up and/or give up their rooms to their visitors. That would be hard with school. Worrying, thinking about it didn't help, so they had hurriedly cleaned their rooms and gone outside. Helping Mason outside gave them the time to open up and ask the questions that had been festering while they cleaned their rooms.

"Dad, are your brother and his family going to stay here? With us?" Mitch asked.

"Where are they going to sleep?" Trenton asked.

"Do we have to give up our rooms?" Brendon added.

They fired the questions at him in the garage where he was sweeping it out.

"Will they like us? Will we like them?" Kyler asked.

"When will they be here?" Aiden wanted to know.

"Whoa, wait a minute. One at a time." Mason stopped his sweeping and addressed their concerns. "They'll probably sleep in the RV or at a motel for some privacy. No one will have to give up his space. You will still have school to prepare for each morning they are here and need your space. I'm sorry you are all worrying about this; we will take care of everything, Mandi, Marty, Carol, and I will handle this.

"I see no reason on earth for you guys not getting along with Chuck and Tonya or them with you. Because of their parents traveling often, they have been home schooled. They have had to adjust to many different cultures and climates. They are very well rounded kids and you will find they can tell you all kinds of stories about their travels. It will be very interesting for all of you."

Mason took a breath, took the time to study each one. They were listening. He continued. "You will like Marty and Carol, too, just fine. Don't worry. They will also like each of you. I do, you know," he smiled.

Okay, he was relieving their tension, somewhat. "And, they should be here within the hour, since I found out Marty's driving. Let's get the vans back into the garage, and take a break to relax." The keys were in the vehicles and he let Mitch and Kyler pull the two vans in.

Mandi pulled in behind them with the groceries to make the noon meal. Brendon carried in the sack for her and offered to help. She had him fill a large pot with water and put it on to boil.

"Salt the water, please," she told him.

"Huh?" he said.

Mandi smiled. "You've never added salt to water on the stove before," she guessed.

"Uh, no. Why do you do that? And how do you know how much to salt the water?" Brendon questioned.

Patiently, she explained, "The salt helps the manicotti not stick together when it is cooking. And, I just salt the top of the water like this," she demonstrated.

"Sorry, I've never done any of this before," Brendon told her.

"There's a first time for everyone; no problem. Thanks for helping."

"Have I been replaced, love?" Mason teased, patting Brendon on the back.

Brendon could tell Mason was teasing. The man opened the refrigerator and started pulling out water bottles and passing them around. He even handed Mandi one.

"Thanks, love, and, no, you have not been replaced. You are too important to replace, even if I have to make this huge dish for lunch." Mason laughed, stopped her from what she was doing and kissed her long and deep. They were both affected and it showed. "What do you need me to do, chop the onion, tell me? Put me to work, woman; I'm yours."

When the two large casseroles were in the oven, Mason headed everyone to the front porch to wait for their company and the lunch.

Marty found the address easily enough. It definitely looked like a family neighborhood, he surmised. He pulled all the way up to the garage door and turned off the car. "Ready, Carol. What does this remind you of?" he asked.

"Ready, Marty, and this looks like where you two grew up. I'll bet the homes are crawling with kids." She grinned and opened her door. Their offspring were faster.

Tonya ran to her aunt and uncle. "I missed you guys soo much," she dragged out, hugging them both. Chuck wasn't far behind his sister. He was embarrassed to hug his aunt and uncle in front of these guys he didn't know yet.

"You're looking good, Chuck," Mason said, seeing his embarrassment and not commenting on it.

Chuck shrugged, said "Hi," as he backed out of his parents' way.

"You're looking good, brother," Marty said. "Americans will always look good to me." He added as he hugged his brother.

"I knew it wasn't just me, Marty," Mason laughed.

Carol shook her head at her husband's comment and hugged her sister-in-law, then Mason.

"Hey, baby, how are you?" Marty asked as he hugged Mandi.

"We are great, Marty; it is good to see all of you."

"Carol, I've always felt sorry for you, putting up with Marty," Mason teased. "It's good to see you've kept him in line." He winked at her.

"It hasn't been easy." She replied. Behind them, Chuck and Tonya were grinning. They had heard all these lines before. They were interested in the other teens standing there on the porch.

"Watch it, woman, or I'll have to take you back to the car." Marty warned his wife; Carol ignored him.

She had her own agenda. "Come on, Mason, introduce us to these good looking guys."

"My pleasure." He did. "Mitch…Kyler…Brendon…Trenton…Aiden." Mason took his time introducing each one of these guys as individuals. Each one said, "Pleased to meet you. Welcome." None of them stepped forward, though.

Carol eyed them. They knew she was watching them also, but discovered it wasn't for the reason they thought. "They don't hug?" She turned to the five pairs of eyes watching her. To them she said, "This family hugs." Slowly they let her hug each one.

Mandi watched each one, judging their reactions. They were uneasy, but okay, too. Carol was an easy person to like and Mandi was sure they would be won over by her friendliness and openness.

"Shall we go inside? Lunch is ready." Mandi offered. Mitch and his brothers had brought up a card table from the basement that she had added to their dining room table to make room for all of them. The table was set for the eleven people to eat comfortably.

"The downstairs bathroom is this way, if you wish to wash up first," Mason told their visitors as he held the door open for them, and pointed toward the bathroom. His niece put her arm around his waist and stayed close to her uncle.

"You get prettier every year," he told her. "I see your braces are off."

Carol followed Mandi into the kitchen, washing up in there, and helping her carry out the food.

"We will be in the states for maybe six months. Christmas will be great this year." Carol mentioned as they carried food and drinks to the table.

"Randie is coming here. I haven't said anything to Mason and Marty's parents yet, but I'm pretty sure they will come. You four have to come, now that you are in the states. You have to," Mandi said.

"That's how we've always done it when we could," Carol answered. "I'll give Marty the order." She laughed.

"You did tell her what I wanted, I see," Marty remarked, his nose telling him what they were having. "And what are you giving me orders for, dearest?" her husband teasingly asked.

Carol let her husband's question slide as her son spoke up, "As long as it is NOT fish or rice, I'm happy, " Chuck said. Carol smiled; she knew both of her children were tired of fish and rice. She was, too.

"I promise you no fish or rice while you are here, Chuck," Mandi pleased him with her statement.

"Thanks, Aunt Mandi, I've lost weight. I really appreciate it." Chuck grinned at her.

"Sit and be quiet, boy," his father told him good naturedly. "You teach them to walk and talk and then you have to tell them to sit and be quiet. Does that make sense to you?" Marty said to Mason as they took their own seats.

Mason looked at Marty, a sly grin on his face. "Do you want me to remind you of when we were their ages?" Mason asked, knowing the answer beforehand.

"Oh, heaven's no, I do not want to repeat or remember any of that." Marty laughed. "I'm very glad I made it through unscafed." Marty left much to the imagination.

"Did you dear?" Carol asked him.

"Until I met you I was lost in the valley of lonely souls" he professed. His two offspring laughed.

Marty had a serious look on his face as he spoke to his wife who just looked at him solemnly. She knew him; he knew it. His whole family knew him.

Mason was laughing as hard as his niece and nephew. Marty eyed him sideways. "You doubt me?" he demanded straight faced.

"I was there. Did you forget that?" Mason spit out, still laughing.

Watching these two close look-alike brothers, the five newcomers to the family were very interested in how they interacted. Chuck and Tonya were used to the camaraderie, but the others weren't, and their eyes and ears were open and attentive.

"Traitor," Marty called him. "Let's partake of this delicious entrée, Mason say the blessing, I'm starved.'

Mandi and Carol looked at each other, and at their husbands. They were used to the interchange.

Mason stilled his laughter, said the blessing, and they ate and listened to tales of France and England, as Marty had spent twenty months total in both places before returning to the states. "We will be in the states for at least six months, near the old homestead even," Marty finished.

He surprised the youth he had just met by saying, "I'll bet it hasn't changed much since you were there." He was speaking of one of the cities he had just finished describing.

"A country like that changes so slowly," Carol added.

"When were you there, Dad?" Mitch asked. Until then, Marty and Carol had not heard the boys call Mason "Dad" or Mandi "Mom." You could see it register on their faces. Mitch did not want to let it bother him, but it did, a little. He kept his eyes on Mason.

"It's been quite a while; I'd have to look up dates. Mandi?" Mason looked to her for her memory to confirm, if she could.

"I am not your computer, dear," Mandi quipped.

"Did you own something there, or do you still?" Trenton asked.

"Did-sold it, Trenton," Mason answered him.

The rest of the meal was the same with Marty answering questions as Mason and Mandi always had, openly, easily. The two brothers definitely were alike in their straightforwardness and in their teasing. Chuck was as easy going as his parents and his new cousins found him willing to befriend them and welcome them into the Morgan clan.

After the meal the teens gravitated out to the field and soon it was full of teens of all ages, all of them guys. The girls in the neighborhood seemed to congregate at each other's houses, not in the field. Tonya was content to be with her mom and aunt. Mason and Marty headed back to lawn chairs on the front porch where they could talk freely. They did. Mason filled his brother in on their sister and all that had happened in the time Marty and his family were out of the country.

"You're really happy, aren't you Mason?" Marty asked.

Mason nodded. "I am, really am. Other than Mandi, they are the best thing to happen to me," Mason admitted.

Mason could always confide in his older brother. They had always been close, once the four years that separated them as children became less prominent.

"Tell me about Randie and Ryan; mom was too upset to make much sense when we called her. We will go by there when we leave here." Marty knew he could get the honest truth from his brother.

Mason did. He related all he knew and ended with Randie planning on coming to Riverton for Christmas. So, he invited Marty and his family to join them. "Do you think we can coerce mom and dad into coming?" Mason watched his brother's face.

"You got me there, bro, I'm not sure, but I'd hope so. I'll help you work on that." Then Marty changed the subject. "Have mom and dad met these guys yet?"

Mason shook his head, and looked across the yard at the field where almost all the neighborhood male teens were congregated. "I haven't taken them out there yet, because of school. I wanted to reestablish their routine and give stability; I wanted them to grow accustomed to us first before carting them off to Billings."

Marty studied his brother. "Should I find something in that statement about me?"

Mason smiled. "No, for two reasons. One, I want them to meet my family and become a real part of our whole family or I would have told you not to come here yet. You know that. Two, you have had your own children from birth and therein is you stability with them. You and Carol are as stable and down to earth as they come, Marty." Mason meant it as a compliment and Marty caught it.

"Thanks. Sometimes I wonder if it was the right way to raise these two. They seem well adjusted and happy." Marty mused, speaking from the heart. His eyes went to the group of teens playing touch football, running, laughing. His son was right in the middle of them as if he lived on this street, too.

Marty grinned. "They like football, huh? Lucky for you."

"You cornered that one. You know I keep waiting for a wall to come up where we butt heads, but so far that hasn't happened."

"It will, Mason, you know that. We butted heads with each other and dad quite a few times, I remember. Chuck and I do once in a while. But Tonya, wow be glad you don't have a girl," Marty told his brother. They both laughed.

As the brothers visited and watched the neighborhood of kids, laughing and running up and down the field, they found more common ground now that both had families.

"I am glad for you and Mandi. You were getting too settled with each other and work-you needed an eye opener." Marty spoke words he had never dared voice before.

"You can give Mandi all the credit. She came up with this vacation plan, and we took an RV out, not having any idea our future would be permanently altered. Life can sure twist you around and spit you out, and wow, you are a new person. These guys had lost their parents, and we found us a family. This will be our home for at least five years until Aiden graduates from high school, I believe."

"You know, Mason, I agree. Every time I get sent out of the country with my job, I wonder what's in store for all of us. So far, it has been worth it."

Mason nodded. "I want to change the subject a minute, Marty: that RV has three bedrooms and the beds are very comfortable. It'll give you privacy and let you rest as the kids are getting up for school on Monday. You're welcome to use it while you're here."

Marty nodded. "It's up to Carol, sounds fine to me. We talked about a motel to give you and us the privacy, but hadn't registered yet."

The door opened and the subject he was referring to walked out.

"Lemonade, guys," Carol offered.

"Thanks," they both answered, taking the offered glasses.

Mason repeated the offer to Carol. "Mandi beat you to it, bud. That will be fine."

"Where are Mandi and Tonya?"

"We're coming, keep your shirts on, jocks," Mandi teased.

"You're never going to outlive that nickname, brother," Marty laughed.

Their laughter could be heard by the guys in the field as they were planning a play. The adults spent almost the whole afternoon on the porch reconnecting and sharing their experiences. The teens spent it running up and down the field. So, guess who was hungry and thirsty?

"Water," she told them when one of them mentioned pop. "You need to replenish your water intake, guys."

Kyler rolled his eyes. "You guys are related." He shook his head.

"Get me the hose. I'll take care of their water intake," Mason said.

"I'll help you," Marty offered.

"Oh, great," Trenton groaned.

Sidestepping the males, the teens headed for the kitchen. They each drank a glass of water so that they could say they had, and then poured themselves milk and raided the cookie jar, emptying it. When the cookies were gone and two glasses of milk apiece, they were ready for more activity.

The rest of the weekend went by quickly with the adults together and the teens together until Sunday evening Mason asked if they would all like to go out on the town.

"If this is anything like our home town, sure, I can handle it," Marty said.

"But, can the town handle you?" his wife remarked. The remark earned her a glare that she ignored.

"I love you, Carol," Mason grinned. The object of his affection didn't believe him for a minute.

"Nice try, but you're usually next on my list," she told him.

Then I know just the place to take you," Mason grinned.

MONDAY

Marty and his family were in the RV as the boys were getting ready for school. Marty and Carol had come over early for coffee and conversation, letting their two sleep in. They had returned to the RV, giving the teens time alone with Mason and Mandi before they left for school.

"Where do Chuck and Tonya go to school when they are in the states?" Aiden asked at breakfast.

"I thought I told you they are home schooled," Mason said, looking up from his computer. "Even here, son, in the states, they are home schooled," he added. "Carol is a certified teacher with a master's in education." He knew that Carol was a very smart lady and a very good teacher, well rounded in how she taught her two children.

With a gleam in his eye, Aiden asked "then can I stay home and have her teach me?"

Mason shook his head, "Sorry, son, that was a good try, but it won't work. You have to go through channels and get registered. And, the answer is

"No," you cannot." Mason watched their youngest's face. Clearly he wanted to stay home with these new relatives, but school came first, was their most important job right now. He meant it whenever he told them how important education was to them and hoped they understood.

"They'll still be here after school, guys, so get moving." Mason teased them. Today he'd made them their waffles again for breakfast while Mandi sat at her end of the table and let Mason wait on them all.

Soon it was Mitch's turn to hurry his brothers up. "Come on, we don't wasn't to be late. Dad might ground us," Mitch added. Everyone could tell he was teasing.

Mason laughed. "I haven't done that yet, have I? Don't worry; I'm sure I'll find a use for it. Bye, guys, Have a good day."

He heard groans on their way out to the garage, plus "Way to go," from Kyler to Mitch as they left. Mason and Mandi looked at each other and laughed.

Marty and his family stayed for the whole week and the next weekend before they left with a promise that they would be back at Christmas. Carol told the boys that now that they were part of the Morgan family and that was forever. She laughed and told them that was what she was told sixteen years ago.

"I like your brother," Mitch confessed as they were watching the family pull away. Mason smiled.

"I knew you would, Mitch, I believe I told you that before they came." Mason was happy that the boys and Chuck had bonded well and that his older brother approved of what he and Mandi had done.

Chapter 9

A MONTH LATER

"What are you looking for?" Kyler asked as the boys all trooped in from school.

Mandi had all the upper cabinet doors open, and she had clearly searched through them. She was standing on a stepstool in the pantry. Hearing Kyler's voice, she stepped down. "Well, guys, Thanksgiving is coming and I'm looking for a pan to cook the turkey in."

"Aiden didn't know where to find one and, so, I'm trying to find one big enough."

"Mom, there's a big roaster pan in the garage in its box. That's what we used," Mitch told her.

"Thank you, Mitch. I made fresh cookies for you guys. They are still on the counter." She smiled at how their eyes lit up at the mention of fresh cookies, and their grins, well they were from ear to ear, surely. Each one headed to the kitchen counter to see who'd get first choice. "They are all the same, I believe," Mandi teased.

Mitch hung back, "I'll get that box down for you, if you want me to." He offered. Mitch understood Mandi's feelings about their first thanksgiving as a new family. He and his brothers had talked about how they would celebrate this traditional feast. Did they want it to be almost like their old ones with their biological parents or did they want something completely new?"

"Yes, thank you, Mitch."

After he got it down, Mitch helped himself to a stack of cookies and a glass of milk, then went to do his homework.

Dinner was over, but no one had left the table yet. Mandi asked all of them to take their plates to the kitchen, to refill their drinks if they wanted, and return to the table. When they did, they noticed she had a notebook and pencil in front of her. She was ready for something, but what?

"What are we doing now?" Kyler asked for all five of them. They'd made lists for her before, so what was she up to now?

"We are making our Thanksgiving menu, young man, one that is for all of us." Mandi began.

"Have you ever cooked a turkey before?" Brendon asked before she could say anymore. As he asked the question the others looked at him, and then at Mandi for her answer.

Mandi meant to reassure them. "Yes, I have. It's been a while, but I have. We ate last Thanksgiving at Mason's parent's home. We were all there for the whole preparation and clean up. Okay? Guys, I do believe you will all live through this." Mandi laughed. "Now I want to know what pies you want me to make, and yes I do know how to bake. I want to know what vegetables you want, how you like your dressing made. The dressing I may not be able to copy, but I'll try."

"Mom, we don't expect you to copy how our mom used to do it. Honest. We are willing to eat whatever you cook. Don't we usually? We are not picky eaters, you know that." Mitch told Mandi. He was serious.

The others offered their comments to Mitch's. "Mitch is right," Trenton said.

"We just like to eat," Brendon added. "You should know that by now. Haven't we eaten everything you and dad cooked so far? Even veggies, right?"

"Okay, let's go about this differently." Mason spoke up. "We want to make out a menu. Will you help us to do that by suggesting some ideas, please?"

"Yes, sir, Dad," Kyler saluted Mason, laughing. Mason reached over and popped Kyler in the back of the head lightly, also smiling.

"We are getting nowhere, and I sure hate the thought of spending the rest of the evening here at this table," Mandi said, sighing loudly.

"Huh? You're kidding, right?" Aiden wrinkled up his face at her. "We have to sit here until you get a menu? Well, I'll do it for us, fast. Pumpkin and pecan pies," he began.

"Hey, I like cherry," Trenton called out.

"Okay," Mandi smiled, "three pies:pumpkin, pecan, and cherry. What else?"

Mitch rolled his eyes, "Mom always made the dressing with bread she broke up and set out for a while to dry it out some. She made a huge bowl of it because we all like it , even as a left over the next day or so. I don't know all she put in it thoough."

"Thank you, dear ," Mandi cooed, teasing. "I want more," she added, looking at the other two who had not spoken yet.

Brendon shrugged, "I don't remember anything else, just the same thing everyone else has: turkey, dressing, mashed potatoes and gravy .Doesn't every family do that , and pie, of course?" Brendon asked of Mandi.

Mandi nodded. "Mostly, yes, that and candied yams with marshmallows. Have any of you ever had them?" she asked. "And salad, maybe, and condiments of some kind, you know-pickles,olives, raw veggies. Would you try any of them, if I fixed them?"

"Of course we will," Mitch assured her. "And we've had yams before. They're okay," he shrugged.

"Can we go now?" Kyler asked, his voice finally heard.

Mandi narrowed her eyes at him. Go, she thought. "What is your favorit part of Thanksgiving, Kyler?" Mandi asked of Kyler, demanding his attention.

"Football," he assured her, looking at Mason. He knew they all their new dad 's love of football.

Mason laughed. "Okay, go, all of you." He ordered. They left the table as quickly as theyy could.

They didn't miss Mandi's cry of "Mason!"

They didn't see him stand and pull her to her feet.

They didn't see them embrace and kiss.

When they could pull apart and talk, Mason told her, "This is our Thanksgiving and we will make it memorable. And,all five of our guys will be happy. You'll see," he promised his mate.

And, he was right. Together, they made up a menu of their own, including three different pies, turkey with dressing, mashed potatoes and gravy, the fresh vegetable tray,and drinks everyone liked. She skipped the regular salad as they had that two nights before with spaghetti.

Everyone swore it was the best Thanksgiving meal they had ever eaten.

And, of course,the TV and the football were the central part of their day, even Mandi's.

"Tomorrow we'll talk about Christmas," Mandi warned the boys. Everyone of them groaned.

"You're ruining the evening, Mom," Mitch stated. "This game is really close." He gave her a sideways look without actually taking his eyes off the TV.

"Mom, come on, please," Kyler groaned.

"Can we just make a list of what we want for Christmas?" Brandon added.

"As long as it's a detailed list of traditions old and new, then I'll think about presents. Maybe," she teased.

"Mom, " Trenton amost whailed as he tried to pay attention to the game.

"Mom," Brendon spilled out the word in distress.

Mason came to their rescue. "Mandi, I promise you a full fledge rebellion if you don't relax, woman. Now!" He rose up from his seat beside Trenton and went to the chair she was occupying-picked her up and kissed her. Then , he sat in that lounge chair with her on his lap

"Now, be quiet, woman, until we are ready for more desert," he ordered her, wiggling his eyebrows. She stared at him, burst out laughing, and then she snuggled down on his lap and sighed, contented.

"I'm in heaven, Mason, you know that, don't you?" she said, very quietly.

He nodded, "Me, too, babe; now shush, the game's back on."

"Yes sir, " she whispered.

THE NEXT DAY

"This is the biggest shopping day of the year, dear. I'm going to join the throngs of the nuts out there and leave you to handle the homefront. Think you can handle that, dear?" she teased.

Mandi was up very early, out of the shower, dressed, ready to shop. Mason was just waking up. The rest of the house was quiet.

Mason couldn't believe his ears. "Okay, love, what have you done with my wife?"

"Mason, I love you, but…let me up. Oh, I love you. Poor darling. Think you can handle it without me today." She teased as she slid off the bed.

"Oh, yes, we will be fine." Mason promised. "Go shop." He laughed as she left the room and he left the bed, heading for the shower.

Dressed, he headed to the kitchen, stirred up waffle mix, ready to cook, made his coffee and poured himself a cup, set the table, then started frying bacon-all before the boys wasdered into the kitchen.

"Where's mom?" Trenton asked.

Mason eyed the lad and said simply, "Shopping. Don't ask me what for, unless you guys have already given her lists I don't know about."

"She…uh…made all of us make a list," Trenton admitted, snatching a slice of cooked bacon.

"Watch it, boy," Mason teased. "She did , huh? Went along with her lists, did she? Well, that's Mandi, she was always great at making lists. I wouldn't expect anything less of my woman. So… that means we are on our own, and I have breakfast about ready."

He poured waffle mix into the cooker and removed the bacon to a platter. "Pour drinks for everyone, Trenton, please,"

That evening, near supper time, Mason had meat ready for tacos and the fixings in the refrigerator to go along with he heard Mandi return . He met her as she climbed the front porch steps.

"Have fun, dear? What did you find? How much are we endebted for?" He flung the questions at her, hoping to catch her off guard. She didn't waver She was wiser than he ave her credit for. So of course, he was exasperated.

"What do you mean you're not going to tell me how much you spent or what you bought? This is not at all like you. We are always open. I want to know why you are keeping me in the dark?" Mason demanded of Mandi upon her return.

"Listen, mister, I'll let you in when I'm ready," she teased, kissing him, preventing any comment. "They all stay in the car'as trunk until I'm ready to bring them inside.

Mason had been outside with their guys working on putting up some Christmas lights and decorations before the snow could hinder them doing so when he and the boys saw her drive into the driveway that evening.

"Don't you want help unloading?" Mitch offered.

She wasn't fooled, no way," Not by a long shot, bud. And, what makes you think I have a whole lot to carry in?" she teased. *"Inside, I need some hot chocolate and sustinence after all that workout." She smiled and she linked her arms with the first two near her, Mitch and Mason. The others followered, shucking off outerwear and shoes to fill the kitchen with bodies and voices.*

"After you've warmed up, you need to see all the decorations we've put up lit up," Aiden told her, excited.

"I didn't know we had so much," Brendon commented. "Maybe we didn't put it all out every year; only mom and dad would know that, not us,' he added, helping himself to a cup of hot chocolate.

Hot soup and sandwiches disappeared as they all talked about the next few weeks: when school ended and vacation started. When they each got to shop for their sibs. When Mason and Mandi would let them have an idea of what to buy them for Christmas. When their new grandparents would arrive. When. When. When. They had a lot of whens to contemplate. And, each of them were very important to all five of them.

The adults tried to address each when as honestly as possible.

An Accidental Family

"I have no idea of anything I need or want," Mason announced, studying their faces. "A new laptop, maybe, but you guys can't pick that out," he finished.

"NO way, bud, the one you are using now was new before we left on our vacation last spring," Mandi vetoed his suggestion.

"Hey," Mason objected, half heartedly, making the guys laugh at their antics.

"You made us make lists, Mom, it's only fair that you do the same," Mitch stated calmly for himself and his brothers.

"You're right," she agreed, rising from her chair at the table. They seemed to spend a lot of time at the dining room table-eating, talking, playing games, making decisions together. Mandi was happy. She knew they wanted to buy gifts for her and Mason as well as each other. She went to the china cabinet drawer and withdrew paper and pens for each of them. Passing them out, she instructed them to think of gifts around twenty dollars apiece.

"It's not about a big price ticket, guys," she told them. "You, too, Mason, start writing," she added to her mate. "It's about sharing and giving. Make your lists. I'll copy them so everyone has a copy and we will keep track of what each of you buy and eliminate duplicates. We can do this, right?"

Kyler's mind was a whirl. "Mom, what if we put three choices on one list and give it to one of us, and put three more choices on another sheet for someone else. There won't be any doubles that way," he finished.

Mason eyed the lad curious, "You have that big a list, son?" Mason asked. "I'm in trouble. Actually, you are, okay?" He laughed.

"CD's don't cost that much, Dad, and I can think of at least four I want," Kyler alerted him. He was in favor of the request he had made and was sure he could convince his brothers of that, if their new parents agreed.

Mason shook his head. Oh, yes, he was new at this. He'd bought for his nieces and nephews, but this was totally new to him. "Okay," he agreed, "We will do it your way, if that is how your brothers feel, also."

Mandi stood watching each one think and write. They all had decided to take their brother's suggestion. Pretty smart thinking, Kyler, she thought as each one made their lists. She was having her own trouble making her lists, because there wasn't anything she really wanted, but understood the boys wanting to buy them gifts to show their feelings.

Mason made two suggestions on each of his sheets, and found it very hard to do even this. He, too, understood their sons' feelings. This was a big new sensation for all of them. He groaned as he made his lists. Quietly. But, Mandi heard. She understood his dilemma.

The hard part over, the list making; the boys were ready to shop. It was on their minds as something new.

"When can we go? How do we do this-without anyone knowing what we have chosen?" Brendon wanted to know.

"That's what I want to know, too?" Kyler added his voice to his brother's.

"Me, too," Aiden said.

Mason held his hand up for quiet. He had an idea. "Okay, this is how we will do this. Mitch, you may drive yourself, just tell us where you are heading and we will keep our distance. Sound fair to you?" When Mitch nodded, he continued, "Kyler, you and Brendon will go with me and buy for everyone but each other. Trenton and Aiden will go with Mandi and buy for everyone but each other. We will meet at that pizza place you all like so well, and have lunch. Then Mandi and I will switch only one and finish the shopping. Can we do this all in one day? If not, we will finish it next week. Sound reasonable to all of you?"

"Except for buying for you two," Brendon said.

"How can we finish in one day?" We've never done that before," Trenton remarked.

"Then we will do whatever needs to be done and however long it takes. We have plenty of time before Christmas. Come on, guys, work with us," Mandi grinned.

"Yes, ma'am," Mitch said, as he grinned at her. His brothers all nodded their willingness to cooperate. Five pairs of eyes were on Mandi. Five pairs of eyes relaxed-a little.

"What do we do about your family coming? Do we buy gifts for them?" Mitch wanted to know. Since they did not know Mason's family, buying for them was a very difficult thought.

"Let's do one thing at a time," Mason assured him, standing up, stretching. He glanced at his wife. "It has already been a very long day for Mandi. And… don't we wonder what she has in the car still?' He wiggled hi eyebrows at her, taking a few tentative steps in her direction teasingly.

"You will have to wait, sir, just as everyone else, Mr. Jock," Mandi told him, stopping his progress with her hand on his chest.

He smiled, looked down at her hand, and then slowly back up at her face. His smile changed. She saw the change. She knew that look, knew she was in for some fun. His chest heaved as he took a noisy long breath. One hand came up and covered her smaller one, capturing it to his chest. His free hand went to the hair at the nape of her neck. Slowly. His eyes were on her alone. He paid no attention to the watchers around them. She was his only interest now.

Her eyes watched him approach her and her hand felt his heart beat as she touched him. She hadn't any desire to remove it even before he covered it with his own. She licked her lips very slowly, the movement not lost on Mason.

"You know," he grinned. "I am very glad you talked me into this vacation. Are we still on vacation, my love?" His eyes twinkled with amusement as he caught her off guard.

She cocked her head to the right, fully aware that five teenagers were still sitting near, their ears wide open as were their their eyes. Five teens who until they met Mason and Mandi did not know that married couples could and did still act like teenagers dating hot and heavy, at least sometimes. Not all couples, mind you, as they had spent time at their friends' homes overnight many times and saw how those parents reacted.

But, they were becoming accustomed to these two showing their affection openly in front them. Still they watched, interested. That affection never went beyond a deep kiss, a tight close hug with hands sprayed on each other's backs, and a few teasing sexual remarks. The boys were all sure that these adults were very active when everyone had retired for the evening. There their young imaginations were overactive. So, now they watched, enjoying the new parents' show in front of them. Yes, they watched. Yes, they each hoped to find mates someday like Mason had, mates they could love as Mason loved Mandi and who loved them as Mandi loved Mason. Wholly. Completely.

Their watching meant Mason and Mandi kept it clean, kept it to a couple kisses and those teasing remarks they loved to exchange. As they were now. Mandi stepped closer sliding her arms slowly up the outside of his shirt toward his neck. He leaned forward and captured her lips; they kissed briefly a couple times-chaste little teasing kisses that promised more to come.

Licking her lips once more, she said, "Vacation. Hmm. Yes, I do believe we are still on a sort of vacation-a working one, my love. And…we shall stay on this vacation for quite a while if I have anything to say about it," she ordered, a smile lighting up her face.

He only laughed and hugged her close. Her arms went up around his neck automatically as she hugged him back.

"So, Christmas shopping is on today's agenda. Then grocery shopping, I suppose," Mason commented. "I'd better go rob a bank," he grinned, teasing.

"Very funny," Mandi quipped.

"Hey, that's what dad always said every year because of Christmas and two birthdays." Mitch laughed at the memory. His brothers joined in.

"I haven't even contemplated birthdays yet. Uh oh, I'm off to the bank for real." Mason said. He left them laughing as he really did check their account on the computer. He knew each boy would need their own money to do his own shopping. Withdrawing that amount would need to be done before they left to shop. Mandi told him they would not do any more shopping today as she was not ready for that yet. They would go on Saturday, giving Mason time to arrange for each to have enough money for the excursion.

SATURDAY

Eight A.M., Mason and Mandi were up, showered, dressed, and downstairs in the kitchen. Breakfast was being prepared: scrambled eggs-two dozen-and toast-the whole loaf, of course. Everyone came in to delicious smells as they were hungry and excited about the shopping trip. During the meal, Mason asked Mitch where he planned to do his shopping.

"The Southland Mall, I think, if that's okay," Mitch answered.

"Of course. I intend to go a different direction at least until lunch. Where are we eating, guys?" Mason asked.

"I thought you said we were going to meet at the Pizza Parlour we've been to a few times," Kyler said.

"Pizza," Mason groaned. "Is that all you guys think about?" He was smiling as he finished his words, taking any sting out of them.

"Yeah, why not?" Kyler asked innocently.

Mason just shook his head, looked at the ceiling, then over at Mandi. He went back to the original subject. "Which way are you heading, love?" he asked, not answering Kyler's objective question. Kyler was watching, smiling.

Mandi named another shopping center for her with Trenton and Aiden.

Mason said, "Let's move out. You are with me right, Kyler?" His look said he hadn't forgotten about his son's comment about the pizza.

Kyler's smile didn't waver; he felt secure with Mason, so he just nodded, stood up and followed Mason out to the vehicle.

Mandi gave everyone a dark shopping bag to hide their purchases so no names would show from the stores they visited and no one could guess what was bought.

They shopped all morning, met at the Pizza Parlour by noon, starved, they said, but managed to talk through the meal before leaving and finishing up what they could.

"I don't know how they found time to eat." Mason complained good-naturedly, noticing all the pizza had disappeared.

With Mitch's help, Mandi found birthday gifts for Kyler whose birthday was December first, and for Brendon whose birthday was December nineteenth. She found Trenton something also, more by accident, but Mitch said he'd really like it, and his birthday was next after Kyler's and Brendon's. She had to keep that one hidden until Trenton's birthday on January fifth. These gifts made her feel like a well-seasoned mom, not a new one.

Mitch had given the car keys to the vehicle he had driven to Kyler to do some by-himself shopping and he and Aiden had gone with Mandi after lunch. Brendon joined Trenton with Mason to finish up his after lunch. Everyone was surprised that they really found what they wanted to buy for each other in only one whole day of shopping.

They were all very tired and at Mandi's suggestion ate Subway sandwiches for dinner before going home. Even Mason did not object to that. He usually wanted a "real meal" but not tonight.

Mason had never shopped like that before, not even when he and Mandi bought gifts for his family and some employees. He was definitely worn out and a;; he did was follow everyone around at the end. He couldn't have told the others what type of sandwich he had eaten, he just ate because he was hungry and tired.

Technically, he had gone to the bank and chosen five three-hundred-dollar visa cards for the boys to use to pay for their gifts. He had filled all three vehicles with gas. And, of course, he had paid for all the meals. But, he was free from the shopping per se because all he had to buy for was Mandi and he already knew what he was buying her. He only supervised the ones he shopped with.

It was Aiden who told his brothers about Mason's gift for Mandi when they were all heading upstairs to their rooms. "You have to see what dad bought mom: this fancy necklace and earring set. Wow, they are so beautiful! Mom will love them. Boy, were they expensive!" Aiden's eyes almost popped out just telling his brothers about the gifts. "The store wrapped them for him. Tell them, Trenton, remember."

Trenton agreed with Aiden. "I was looking to see if I could afford anything for my girlfriend, but that place was to expensive for me. Mom and dad must be very rich if they can afford to give us three-hundred dollars apiece and he still buy mom a gift like that. Haven't they paid for all of our expenses since they met us? "He looked at Mitch for conformation on that statement.

"I will bet that the money he gave us to spend on each other didn't come out of that account dad set up for us last summer." Mitch said. As far as he knew, that account had only been used five times, when Mitch paid for his tuition at the beginning of school on registration day, for pizza once, and for power, water, and garbage each only once. Mitch had not used the account again and none of his brothers had ever asked him for money for anything. They always went to Mason or Mandi who always wrote out checks.

One time Mitch had checked out the check book and found only those six checks written. That was when one of his brothers needed money for something, maybe lunches, or maybe it was for Brendon's permit-Mitch couldn't remember now, but before Mitch could do anything, Mandi took care of it.

Before Christmas, Brendon could get his license, and Mitch would bet his lunch money that Mandi or Mason would take him and pay for it out of their money. Kyler and Mitch had had to get new licenses with their new names after the adoption was final and Mason had paid for that, too, of course.

"Did mom buy anything for dad while we were out today? " Kyler asked. "I know she didn't before lunch but we switched places."

Mitch shook his head. "Not when Aiden and I were with her, she didn't, I know. She was more interested in us getting everything we needed to get done." Mitch spoke for all of them.

Mandi collected all their lists after they were through shopping so she knew who had bought what for whom as it was clearly marked off. She was honest enough not to ask for her lists and didn't care to know about it. Using the boys' lists as a guide, she made one of her own of what hadn't gotten bought for each by their sibs. They would get everything on their lists this year because she intended to spoil each of them-happily. She would have help-her in-laws called and wanted to bring gifts for the boys when they came for the holidays. She had the list she had made. Randie called. They were coming also and she needed ideas. Mandi had the list. Marty and Carol would arrive on the twenty-third and wanted ideas. She had the list.

Usually she and Mason bought one personal gift for each other and then bought a piece of furniture or some big item they needed or wanted-together. She supposed it would be the same the same this year.

Chapter 10

The second Saturday in December, she took the boys shopping again, for all of Mason's extended family. They needed gifts for them, too. Mason joined them after a business meeting via his computer with a couple companies they owned. The adults gave advice on what to buy and they made the purchases. Afterwards, Mason announced, "No pizza today, guys. I'm hungry and I want real food." He told them "Today we go to that diner I saw around the corner." Mason was pleased that the boys placated him by not complaining. No one went away hungry, not Mason, particularialy.

For Randie's children, David, the oldest, they bought a model airplane set, and for Julie, they found a game, while for the youngest, Gina would love her new doll and stroller set. Mandi chose a football for David from her and Mason and a pink dress for Julie, She found a dishes set for Gina. A sweatshirt in Randie's favorite color-light green with navy trim-was the perfect find from all of them. Coming across a key chain that said "Miranda Rules" was the perfect topper for Mason's sister.

"Randie's real name is Miranda?" Kyler asked as Mandi paid for some purchases. She nodded.

She explained, "Mason was the one who nicknamed her Randie when they were very young. She wanted to be one of the boys, run with Mason and Marty and the other boys in the neighborhood. There weren't any girls for her to play with, so she really hadn't any choice, you see. That's the story I got from Mason, anyway," she told them.

"We wondered why her name was Randie when dad's and Uncle Marty's names start with "M's" Kyler stated.

Since Mandi found a couple CD's and a sweatshirt hoodie for Tonya, all they had left to buy for were Marty, Carol, and Chuck. "Mason you have to help us out, not just follow us around," Mandi complained calmly.

"I do, huh?" Mason grinned. "Well, let's see. What in the world would Marty need or want?" He was honestly thinking, so Mandi kept quiet, and didn't interrupt him. "Hey, I think I remember that Chuck wants a new Packer's jersey. Am I helping?" He was grinning, proud of himself.

Mandi gave him a full smile, and said, "Good. You pick it out. Across the way," she pointed, "and we'll go over here. Wait. Actually, you guys all go with Mason. I'm going into this store here and I'm sure none of you want to go with me." The store was a woman's dress store and all the boys were glad she let them off the hook and they could happily go with Mason and let her go there…alone.

This shopping was not as easy as they had thought it would be, not like a couple weeks ago. Too much involvement. Too much thinking about buying for people they did not know. They still had two grandparents to buy for and no clues what they might want. Did the gift have to show how much these guys appreciated their newfound family? No one dared to ask, not wanting to upset Mason.

Also, their real grandparents had called and wanted to see them. As they lived quite a distance away, the boys did not usually see them more than twice a year. The last time had been at their real parent's funeral, when they did not even stay overnight to make sure the boys would be okay. Did they have to buy them gifts, too? Did it seem right to use Mason and Mandi's money to buy gifts for these grandparents that the adults had not even met? Adults who had not called once in six months to make sure the boys were together and doing okay!

In Mitch's eyes, that made him respect Mason and Mandi more and love Mason and Mandi more. Both put the boys first from day one, took them to church on Sundays; Mandi took them to their doctors' appointments, their dentist appointments, cooked, cleaned, did their laundry, in all ways, she took care of them and cared about them. These were the attributes Mitch had learned to appreciate.

Mandi found an outfit for Carol that she was pretty sure would be okay, and went across to the store where the guys were. Mason had succeeded in picking out a jersey and hat for Chuck and another jersey for his brother.

"You are so wonderful," Mandi told Mason in front of the clerk and the boys who were used to her comments by now.

"We knew it, right, Dad?" Mitch said teasingly, a remark which earned him a playful swat from Mandi.

"Grandparents," Mason said exasperated. "What do we buy them? Can we go home and think about this? Otherwise, we are done, right?" Mandi nodded, agreeing with him about going home and thinking about it.

"I'm tired of shopping," Mandi said. She kept a straight face.

Mason's eyes lit up. "Say that again," he teased.

"Watch it," she warned, whispering, "jock" as they exited the store.

Mason just took her package from her, adjusted it with his in one arm, and put his other arm around her, pulling her close. Her arm closest to him slid around his waist and they strolled toward the exit.

They all stopped for a minute, watching some kids with a store Santa. All were definitely in the Christmas spirit, humming along with the piped in holiday music. They headed home to wrap more gifts and enjoy the rest of the weekend.

December first, they celebrated Kyler's birthday as they had Mitch's back in September with dinner out and cake and ice cream at home. Winter was upon them with colder temperatures and snow flurries. Mitchell had turned eighteen in September and was still happy that he didn't have to be responsible for his brothers that they had parents again to take care of them. Now Kyler was seventeen, soon Brendon would be sixteen and would get his license, just six days before Christmas. Sometimes all the events that needed to be attended to still scared Mitch. He had come so close to having to deal with everything by himself, so close to losing his youth and having to act like the adult for and with his brothers. One of these days he was going to have to thank Mason and Mandi for taking that responsibility from him and for him.

"Boy am I glad all the outside decorations are up," Mason announced when he came home from work the day after Kyler's birthday. He was brushing the snow flurries off his face. The car he had driven was the one that stayed outside of the garage. "Can we go home now? I like our warmer weather much better." He walked to her and turned her into his arms away from the stove, hugged and kissed her thoroughly.

Confused, Mason looked around the kitchen. "Are we having company for dinner? Or a party I don't know about?" There were bowls all over the counter: they were filled with dough and Mason was confused. He glanced at the stove again. On it were pans filled with food that looked like the makings of a healthy fulfilling meal. So...Why all the bowls filled with uncooked dough?

Mandi laughed as she stepped out of his arms to attend to the meal finishings. "No, no, dear, no company. I'm mixing up some different cookie recipes for the holidays. Of course, the boys will have to sample some," she told him.

"And, I'm one of the boys, right?" He teasingly winked at her.

They were both laughing when Trenton walked in on them.

"Is supper ready? I'm starved. What's so funny?" Trenton's questions came out fast as he stared at the adults.

"Mason's jealous," Mandi told their son, trying to control her own emotions.

"What?" Mason said his own laughter ceasing.

"What" Trenton echoed staring at them both?

"Just because I want to sample your cookies, too?"

Her smile was smug. "Go set the table, tell everyone to wash up, and we'll eat…dear."

Mason looked sideways at Trenton. Trenton backed up, Leary. What was his dad going to do?

Mandi had turned around to the stove as she talked, turned off the oven and the burners. She yelped as Mason grabbed her and picked her up. Trenton just stared.

"Woman, you are in trouble now," he informed her. "Getting too cocky, I believe. Let's cool you off." He held her close. He headed toward the back door, laughing, kissing her neck and cheek, and then capturing her lips.

The kiss over, "Mason," she gulped out.

"Yes, love," he asked innocently. His smile belied the innocence.

"It's cold outside. Remember you said that when you came in?" Her arms tightened around his neck.

"Yes, I remember," he said too calmly.

"Mason!" Her voice rose as he reached for the door handle.

He laughed at her nervous voice, then let go of the door and set her back on her feet. Her arms were still around his neck.

"You…" she began, but he kissed her long and hard, pulling her as close as he could. The kiss deepened…and deepened…and seemed to last forever.

Trenton called out to them, not the least embarrassed. "Hey, Mom, Dad, we are hungry and you said the food was ready. Do you want us to go ahead and eat without you?" No answer. Had they heard him? Trenton thought not. Shaking his head, Trenton set the table. They were still locked together. He pulled the food out of the oven and off the stove and set them on hot pads on the table.

They were still kissing. Trenton couldn't believe it. He went and called his brothers to eat. They came down ready to eat. As they were all sitting down, Mason and Mandi joined them. They looked thoroughly engrossed in each other. Mason walked Mandi to her seat and pulled out her chair for her, then proceeded to his chair. On the way, he tousled Trenton's hair and clapped him on the back without saying a word.

The others all watched, waited for Mason to sit down and say the blessing so they could eat. He was walking slower than usual. Why?

Mitch looked from his mom to Trenton, and then his eyes followed his dad to his chair. Sitting, Mason gave away nothing. He was calm, happy, smiling.

Before the blessing, Mason commented, "I guess everyone is extra hungry tonight. Did Mandi refuse you snacks after school or something?" All eyes were on him but no sound reached his ears. He blessed the food and asked God to bless the family being nourished by the food. He asked God to help them truly learn the meaning of the coming season. Then…"Let's eat," he finished.

A few tentative wondering looks passed back and forth across the table as the food was passed around.

"Dad," Mitch began. He had only taken a couple bites after filling his plates.

"Yes, Mitch," Mason looked over at the oldest teenager

"What gives?" Mitch asked.

Mason raised his eyebrows and studied the young man. The lad was smart but not as smart as his new dad. "As far as I know, nothing gives, unless it's stretchable. So, explain your question a little more." Mason kept a straight face, no smile, no frown.

"Uh, what's happening? Uh, what happened? You know," Mitch declared. "We don't, but want to>" Mitch stared at Mason.

Mason's eyes went from Mitch to Mandi, stayed there a full minute, then to Trenton who was watching him, and back to Mitch. "Nothing has happened, Mitch, 'Mason spoke slowly, "so, eat. I came home. I kissed my wife. I'm having dinner with my family. Those are the important things in life, son. Eat. Enjoy." He winked at Mitch, then gave his attention to the food.

Trenton didn't dare change that; he shrugged, let it drop. Mitch noticed his brother's shrug and he, too, went back to his meal.

SATURDAY

Mason mentioned to Mandi and anyone who would listen, "One thing about this cold weather-the grass isn't growing."

"No dear, it's not, so you can help me today," Mandi answered him, smiling.

He groaned, but grinned then and said, "Okay, woman what do you need?" When she looked at him, he had the answer, "I'll take the Kitchen." She thought she knew what he had in mind-cooking. Mason loved to cook much better than he had given the boys any inkling of, as of yet.

Mason cleaned the kitchen as he had messed it up making a big pot of beef vegetable soup for lunch and dinner. For him this was a great lunch and dinner meal, but the boys might not agree. Mason didn't know how the boys felt about vegetable soup, but he would soon find out.

That afternoon Mason talked to his sister, Randie, and told her to bring the kids out to stay with them for the whole Christmas vacation as soon as school was out. She could spend the whole time with them and get to know the boys that he and Mandi had adopted-boys he easily admitted to her had stolen their hearts. He knew they could make room and Mandi sure wouldn't care. Over supper he related to Mandi his talk with Randie. Mandi said he was right to invite her. She looked at their sons and saw mixed emotions on the five teen faces. She tried to reassure them.

"Hey, it's going to be fine. Really. Randie is a great lady. I really like her and her kids. You guys will too. Honest. Take my word for it." Mandi hoped her words were helpful.

"Uh…can I ask you something? It's important or I wouldn't change the subject." Mitch knew that was what he was doing, but he needed to bring another subject out in the open. He did not intend to be the cause of an argument. Not for what he had to tell Mason and Mandi.

"Of course you can. Mitch," Mason answered, "You already know that."

They were all sitting at the table still, although the food was almost all gone. The boys had enjoyed the soup and luckily he'd only put half of it on the table. There was still more for lunch tomorrow. Mason was glad it had gone over so well.

This table had been the center of many conversations throughout the ten years it had been in this family, long before Mason and Mandi came here to carry on the tradition they knew nothing about.

Mitch bit his bottom lip, a sure sign of nervousness, and took a breath before looking at Mason. "We had a phone call here at home today, while you and mom were outside. I answered it…" He seemed to choke on the next words, has trouble forming them.

Mason was worried. Was someone harassing Mitch? Or all of these guys? Was someone bringing problems into their lives? And, why? All these things went through Mason's head in the matter of two seconds.

Mitch continued, "The call was from our grandmother on our dad's side. She wants to come by and see us. Over Christmas. She thought…she thought we were living here alone." He stopped.

Mason's thoughts ran in a different direction now. Six months and she was just now calling to visit, not to see how they were doing? His next thought was for Mitch and his brothers. She was still their grandmother even though she had not seen them or contacted them since the funeral. So, he took a minute to process Mitch's words and his own thoughts. He needed to be completely open and ease Mitch's anxiety.

"Mitch, I guess I can understand your nervousness," Mason spoke slowly. "But, my son," Mason added these words as reassurances, " I'd have thought you would know by now that we, Mandi and I, would have NO, capital NO, objections to this grandmother coming here at any time, Christmas or otherwise. Is that understood…by all of you? Aunts, uncles, cousins, and grandparents-they are a part of you and are welcome here. Mason stopped and waited for all of his words to register. He knew this was important and needed to be addressed now for these guys to feel secure.

Mitch looked forlorn, like Mason had knocked the wind out of him with his words. It took a minute for all of his dad's speech to register and when it did seep through his noodle, he had the good grace to feel remorse. "I'm sorry, Dad, really. I just felt torn between… you know…" He shrugged, then began again. "We only see them twice a year- once during the summer and at Christmas. I don't know why I didn't think to mention that to you. They live far away, in Canada and only travel at those times, I guess." He didn't know any other way of explaining this to them. He felt like he had failed.

"Mitch, calm down," Mason ordered calmly. "Is your grandfather still alive?" When Mitch said, "Yes, Sir," Mason continued, "Did you tell them they could come by here? Again Mitch nodded.

"Yes, sir, I thought we'd find a way." He shrugged. "They usually stay at a motel near here, not in the house or they have before. Do they think your bedroom is free for them? Dad, I didn't tell them about you and mom, because they didn't really give much chance to talk. I'm sorry, that sounds like I'm being evasive or like I'm not proud of you and mom, and I am. I love you both-you know that, don't you?"

Mandi spoke for the first time, "First of all, of course there is a way, Mitch. Second, we will find room for everyone to visit and eat, and somehow sleep. Third, we are not upset that they do not know about Mason and me or about the adoption. We will cross that bridge when they arrive. All are welcome. It is Christmas and Christmas is about giving and sharing.

"We will tell them they can visit anytime. Understood?" Mandi was upset that they did not feel comfortable telling her and Mason about the phone call and the upcoming visit.

"Did they leave a number where they could be reached?" Mason asked.

Mitch was relieved that his parents were so willing to accept their grandparents on their biological dad's side. He looked at Mason. "Yes, Sir, I wrote it down. It's by the phone in the family room," Mitch confirmed.

"Thank you, Mitch. Everything will be fine. We will have a wonderful holiday," Mandi promised him and his brothers.

FRIDAY

"School's out," Aiden shouted, almost in Mandi's ear, as he opened the passenger door and climbed into the vehicle. Mandi covered her ears, and smiled; Aiden continued, "I'm free for two whole weeks," he said gleefully as he tossed his bookbag on the floor where his feet were.

"Buckle up, lad, you're not that free, yet," Mandi teased. Mandi drove home listening to the boy chatter as she maneuvered the car through streets she knew very well now. Inside the kitchen, Aiden announced, 'No homework for two weeks!" He filled a plate with cookies and poured himself a large glass of milk after entering. "I'll be in the family room chillin'" he informed her, leaving her rolling her eyes.

Mason was running some errands and would be home soon. They had decided to take the boys out for supper because this would be one of the last days without company during the holidays. Mandi booted up her computer in the same room Aiden was in. The TV did not bother her as she worked on another of their holdings, checking out its progress. This is where the other four teens found her when they arrived jubilant about being out of school.

"You will find out one of these days that school is not so bad," she said to no one in particular, and to all present.

"That'll be the day," Trenton answered.

"Yeah, right," Brendon echoed.

"You're both right," Mandi told them. "There are cookies and milk in the kitchen as usual. We are going out to eat as soon as Mason gets home, so don't stuff yourselves. And, change clothes, if you wish, but be ready when Mason arrives, please." Cookies and milk were more important.

Mandi had baked more cookies in the past six months than in her whole life before. No guess work there with five hungry teens gobbling them up almost as fast as she could bake them. How was she going to keep cookies around for the holidays with their empty stomachs? She'd mix up another batch tonight after they came home to bake tomorrow. And, brownies. She needed to mix up and bake brownies. Mason had mentioned them yesterday.

Mandi's cell phone rang as she turned off her computer. The ID said: Charles Morgan. She smiled, said, "Hello."

"Hello, yourself. Are you ready for the holiday hustle and crowds?"

"As ready as I'll ever be tonight, tomorrow, and the next day. Are you? Marty and Carol will be here in four days, and Randie tomorrow," she told her father-in-law. "When can we expect you and mom?"

"Tomorrow, noon flight, that's why I'm calling. We will be with Randie and her kids. Are you ready, I repeat?" Charles was retired and enjoyed his family. He was a fair man, well liked and respected.

She could hear his reluctance to pile all of them upon her and Mason and five teens he had yet to meet. She could also hear his excitement: the man loved his grandkids to a fault; the five he knew now were his pride and joy. She had no doubt at all that he'd love the five here. Mandi had fallen for Charles Morgan's charm at that first meeting when Mason took her to his home for a weekend visit during her senior year at college. She knew immediately where her future husband learned to be so charming. Charles was an affable character and she was under his spell thereafter.

"I will be there with your taxi and you'll find out how ready we are, Dad. We can't wait." She took a deep breath of happiness as she talked.

"Good thing, girl, because you are being invaded," her father-in-law warned with a laugh. "Till then, bye, and I love you."

"I love you, too, bye." They disconnected. Charles was ready to welcome the sons that his son and daughter-in-law had adopted. Mandi hung up and found Kyler watching her, frowning, a "need-to-know" look on his face.

She kissed his cheek as he stole a spoonful of the cookie dough she was mixing up.

"Gotta test it," Kyler teased. "And, who was that on the phone?"

"Nosy," she scolded, no scolding intended. "That was your grandfather, a really friendly, great guy. He wanted to tell me the time of their arrival. He will be here tomorrow with his wife, your grandmother, another wonderful person, and with Randie and her three children. Remember this: I love them as my own. I love you guys as my own. They will love all of you just as Mason and I do. Mason and I will be here for all of you. But…you will not need any help, nor do you have anything to worry about.

"Now, scoot, so I can get some cookies baked," she shooed Kyler out of the kitchen.

SATURDAY

So far the brothers had spatted or disagreed very little since meeting the Morgans, usually outside and during scrimmaging with friends in the neighborhood. They had been able to resolve their differences without Mason or Mandi knowing or intercepting .Also they wanted to please Mason and Mandi and not scare them away, so they were always on their best behavior.

That was about to change. That was inevitable actually. Teenagers and brothers especially were not immune to disagreements.

Mason drove one minivan and Mandi drove the older one. She had Kyler and Aiden with her and Mason had the other three with him. All five were nervous. The two adults were excited.

Of course they were early in case the flight arrived earlier which it didn't. So, the boy's nerves were on edge. Mason and Mandi had never heard them snap at each other like this before.

"Watch your foot."

"That's my seat."

"Move your arm."

"Move."

"That's mine."

What they were complaining about was not worth the time or trouble, but their nerves were on edge and the adults cold tell.

It went on for about five minutes while Mason and Mandi tried to let them work through it by themselves. They set next to each other and couldn't believe their ears.

Finally: "Kyler, sit over there and don't say another word," Mason ordered harshly. The teen, shocked by Mason's tone moved to the seat without a word.

"Mitch, there, same rule, be quiet," he demanded as he pointed to another bench away from his brothers. Embarrassed, Mitch moved.

"Trenton," He pointed to another chair and Trenton followed his order.

"Brendon, quiet, now and sit here," Mason said.

Aiden was sitting next to Mandi his eyes wide.

Mason continued. "I am outraged at each of you. There is no reason to let worry cause you to pick at each other. I will not allow it. You are better than this. I know you are." Mason scrubbed his face with his hand and then continued, "Everyone relax until the plane arrives. When my parents arrive, then you may stand up and talk again.

He had never really scolded them before. They each knew they deserved it. It didn't take away the anguish over putting him through this. They had fought before and been punished before by their birth parents but this was different. They were too old to be separated out in public like little kids and very embarrassed by Mason doing it. No one said a word. They kept their eyes on the floor or their shoes in front of them quietly.

Mason hadn't any other idea what else to do to ease the tension in each of them. He and Mandi had constantly told them that his family would be happy to meet them. Hadn't they gotten along just fine with his brother and his family? Why would this be any different? Mason sure didn't know. He glanced at Mandi and she smiled at him. What else could he do? Her eyes were reassuring. The hand he held squeezed his.

Most of the time they did get along. The few spats they had had usually were worked out without Mason or Mandi even knowing about them. A few times Mason had called out "Hey" and they'd backed off when they were in the field with their friends, usually running the football; that was all Mason knew about. They were outside playing a game in the field at those times. They were brothers and intended to stick together, but they were also normal teenagers.

One time the whole group of teenagers was scrimmaging up and down the field. They had chosen teams and were facing each other. Aiden was not on his brothers' side during the game. Aiden fumbled the ball and was tackled, by his brother Brendon-hard. He was not happy.

Jumping up he yelled, "I quit. I'm tired of always being last, being tackled." He growled, leaving the field. Leaving his brothers staring at him, worried that Mason or Mandi would be mad at them for doing this to Aiden, making Aiden leave. So far they had tried hard not to let the Morgans see their "bad side."

They didn't realize that Mason and Mandi kept them wondering when they would have to intervene in some dispute, and could not believe it had not happened in the six months they had been together.

That time, Aiden had gone in the front door, didn't spot either adult as he went up to his room. There, he turned on his music and enjoyed the solitude until supper time.

Outside he had left his brothers staring and worrying, until their friends interrupted them with "Hey, come on, let's play." They did, leaving Aiden on his own, and enjoying themselves, until suppertime. The two adults were unaware.

Mandi closed her eyes and her mouth and let Mason handle it. Her eardrums were tired of the confrontations. Her head was starting to pound. She opened her purse and popped a couple pills with a bottle of lukewarm water.

Mason stood up. Her eyes followed him as he bought another bottle of water.

She cast sideways glances at each lad sitting stiffly away from each other, each one looking guilty and contrite at the same time. She wouldn't smile. Her eyes found Mason again as he downed half of the water before rejoining her on her free side.

"Okay, what is wrong here?" he asked his wife as he sat. He meant the boys temperaments. She knew exactly what her husband meant.

"Just nerves, I think. Give them time to meet our guests and they will be fine," she assured him, reaching for his cold water. He released it and she said, "Ahh," as she drank some.

Finally, they could see the plane come taxing down the runway toward the building. Mason stood up and went to the window to watch the people embark. When he saw his family coming down the stairway, and walking toward the terminal, he turned to his sons.

"Come here," he simply said. They all stood up and came to him.

"Dad, I'm sorry."

"Me, too."

"We were wrong."

"I'm sorry."

"Dad, I'm sorry, too."

"Is it okay?"

"Dad?"

The boys had settled down when Mason separated them, sitting, brooding over their actions and his words. What had they done? Would Mason and Mandi forgive them? The minute Mason had called them to him, they had all tried to apologize, and found both him and Mandi forgiving. They were relieved. For that they were happy. But, it didn't erase their anxiety over the people coming off the plane.

Mason smiled. They all fired the apologies at him. He didn't have time to answer until…finally they were quiet. "Of course, everything is okay. I love you guys." His hands reached out and touched shoulders, tossed Aiden's hair, clapped Mitch's shoulder, Kyler's cheek. I love you," he repeated. He looked at Mandi, then at their sons. "Now let's greet our guests."

Mandi was by his side. She felt the teens discomfort, knew they were normal average teenagers. And, they were loved, would always be protected, would have as normal a life as possible- all because of her and Mason. And- she and Mason felt they were the lucky ones.

Charles and Mary Morgan walked into the terminal, saw their son talking to their new grandsons. They were too far away to hear the words, just read the expressions on their son's face: love. That was easy to see.

Charles smiled.

Mason looked up and smiled. He and his dad had a good relationship as adults. All childish behavior was water under the bridge for them. They were two males who enjoyed each other's company.

"Hi, Dad." His right hand was still on Mitch's shoulder He patted the lad's shoulder once more before dropping his hand. The boys all turned and gave Mason room to greet his father and mother.

Charles and Mason shook hands, their other free hand coming to join the clasped ones.

"Good to see you, Dad. Welcome to Riverton."

Mary waited only one minute for them to connect as she hugged Mandi, then her son.

"Mom, you are looking much better than the last time I saw you. I'm glad. You had me worried for a while." Mason said the words sincerely.

"Your dad, too, I guess. He about drove me nuts," she replied as her son kissed her cheek, and then glanced at his sister, Randie.

"How did you hold them at bay?" he teased.

Randie smiled a smile almost identical to her brother's. "I threatened them," she stated.

"Ha. Where's Randie?" Mason returned her teasing.

At the adult's words, the spell was broken. All three children ran to Mason and Mandi. Mason ruffled nine-year-old David's hair and picked up the two-year-old Gina. Mandi hugged the six-year-old Julie close and admired her new outfit. The child beamed, hugging Mandi and stayed near.

The two-year-old put both her hands on her uncle's cheeks after giving him a bear hug. He said, "How's my favorite two-year-old?"

"I'm a fine one, Grandpa says," she announced. Mason kissed her cheek.

Laughing, he said, "You are indeed, squirt." He sat her down and hugged his other niece. "You are getting prettier every day, sweetheart," he told her. Again she beamed.

"How's my favorite sister?" he grinned at Randie.

She guffawed. "I'm your only sister, smartie," she laughed, then hugged her brother, who grinned as he hugged her.

"Sis, you look fantastic," he told her. "Now…" he said. "Time for intros." He put his arm around her waist. Mason then turned his attention to the teens who were quietly watching all the activity. His parents had stood aside as Randie and her three were the center of Mason's and Mandi's attention for a few minutes. They watched the five teens who were watching Mason and Mandi. The boys were nervous; Charles could see that in their demeanor.

So…the teens watched as Mason interacted with members of his family, watched Mason with his parents and saw the shared love. They could also see how much he loved his sister and her kids, and that loved was returned fully. It helped to reaffirm Mason's love for them as he introduced everyone before they all piled into the two vehicles and headed home.

The intros had seemed to take forever, but finally they were over and they were back in their more relaxed atmosphere.

The RV was put back into use as the Morgans extended family deserved some privacy, too. For four days, they spent time getting to know each other. It was different having Mason's family around, but fun, too. Their new grandmother loved to bake and so did their new aunt. Between the three women, there were more than plenty of goodies to sample. They could test to their hearts delight.

Mason was happy to see and know his sister was again in control of her life and her children. He was glad that the lawyer had hired was worth the money and his sister would not lose her family.

Chapter 11

"Mom, telephone," Brendon called out bringing her the extension. He had answered it so he knew who was on the line.

"Thanks," Mandi told him, wiping her hands on a paper towel. She didn't think to ask who it was on the line, didn't think of that, just took the extension and said, "Hello. Yes, this is the Cooke residence or it was. How can I help you?...Oh, yes, we've been expecting your call....You are most welcome. I don't think the Mitch explained the situation to you, but we want you to come by....Yes, anytime is fine....Stay for dinner, of course. Stay as long as you can. We want the boys to be around you. Really...Yes, that will be fine. Bye."

Mandi pushed the end button and laid the phone on the counter to check the brownies she was baking. Another batch of cookies on a sheet replaced the brownies.

Mary studied her. "Who was that?" She stopped mixing up the batch of oatmeal cookies to watch her daughter-in-law's face.

"That was Mr. and Mrs. Cooke, the boy's paternal grandparents. They visit twice a year, Mitch told me, coming down from somewhere in Canada. I told the guys that, of course, they were welcome. You can't have too many grandparents, right. We can't deny them their family."

Mary smiled. "That is very understanding of you. I'm sure it makes the guys feel more comfortable knowing you let them still have contact with this couple, even if they can only come twice a year."

"You know, Mom, I was thinking, we could take them on a trip to Canada sometime, too. Maybe next summer. I want to take them to California to our residence there also, and to Nevada whenever we can arrange all these trips. I'll have to run that by Mason and let you know our schedule."

Mary stopped mixing up the last batch of cookies and eyed Mandi. "You amaze me. You and Mason have taken on a lot and you seem to be doing fine. The guys seem like very good decent young men, and I can see why you and Mason love them. I believe I do already myself."

"I think that those trips would be good experiences for all of us. We've taken on a lot of responsibility with these boys, but we really love them, and would not want it any other way. Both Mason and I feel we are very lucky to have met these guys, and would not have it any other way. We need to learn how to be parents of teenagers. I know we are new at this and the guys have been on their best behavior. Mason and I are going to need some advice at some time, we are both sure of that. So, don't be surprised if and when we call you," Mandi told her mother-in-law as they finished up with the cookies and started on supper preparations.

Mitch turned around and left the kitchen without either woman knowing he had heard anything. He told his brothers that their grandparents, the Cooke's were coming today and staying for Christmas. He told them that he had heard their mother say that she was glad she had met them and become their mom and that their new grandmother loved them already. He knew his brothers were as excited with the news as he was.

Dinner was ready. Mary, Carol, and Mandi had prepared the meal for nineteen people as Randie set the table and made drinks ready. She had spent time with her family, getting to know her new nephews, and visiting with her brothers.

Mason had purchased a second dining room table and arranged it in the dining room by removing the extra furniture so they could all eat in the same room. He planned to store it in the basement for future use.

The boys were in the family room visiting with their grandparents, Peter and Evelyn Cooke, as the dinner was being prepared. The Cooke's had arrived around two that afternoon, and the Morgans had introduced themselves and then left the Cookes to visit with the five teens.

Mandi went to the family room doorway, heard Mitch talking about how good Mason was at football, bragging about the man as his dad. Mitch sounded very proud. She smiled. Listened until Mitch was finished speaking before interrupting.

"Dinner's ready. Anyone hungry?" she announced. She smiled at her sons as proud as if they had been hers from birth.

"I am," she heard at least five times as the teens stood up and faced her, smiling. They were happy to have their grandparents visiting as they always were. They were proud of their new parents and told the Cookes so. They were not embarrassed to be calling Mason "Dad" and Mandi "Mom" and hoped their paternal grandparents could accept that. They all raved about the Morgans to the Cookes during the time spent in that family room. Each one had something to say, a story of what Mason or Mandi had done for them. Each one seemed to be enthralled with their new parents. Each one wanted to please their first set of grandparents and their new family they had inherited.

It was hard for the Cookes to hear their grandsons call another man "Dad" so soon after the death of their son. They themselves had not truly gotten over missing their only son. Besides that, these boys had given up the Cooke name and that took away the succession of the family tree. These were the only grandchildren they had and they feared losing them to this new set of grandparents. They couldn't deny the hero worship they were witnessing and hoped it was not be their only connection with their new parents as adoption was really permanent. By the time their visit was over, they were reassured that their grandsons were better off now than they would have been without the Morgans. They were also assured that the Morgans truly loved these five teenagers and would not desert them as the years passed. They were very happy that the Morgans would be willing to allow them to still see their grandsons twice a year as they did now. The adults became friends during the Christmas season.

No one could deny that having parents was better than not having them. No one could deny that two sets of grandparents was an asset. It seemed everyone benefited. No one complained…now.

Nineteen people sat at the two long extended tables and devoured the meal. Peter and Evelyn watched how all the Morgans related to each other and to how their grandsons were welcomed and accepted and treated as part of this established family. This was truly a blessed Christmas.

www.ingramcontent.com/pod-product-compliance
Lightning Source LLC
LaVergne TN
LVHW091558060526
838200LV00036B/899